The Center for Contemplative shares

THE PLACE NO ONE WANTS TO LOOK

A Lay Cistercian reflects on six questions every human must answer before they die and how using contemplative spirituality allows us to approach the Mystery of Faith.

A Journal Retreat

Michael F. Conrad, Ed.D.

This book may not be reproduced by photocopying without the
permission in writing from the publisher.
The Center for Contemplative Practice
2402 Glenshire Lane
Tallahassee, FL 32309
Printed in the United States of America July 2018
Copyright 2018, All Rights Reserved

As you can tell from the somewhat unique title, I assume that spirituality is innately common to all humans, in the sense that we all search within us for meaning which makes sense to us. Answers to some of the core concepts of what it means to be human and what it means to be a spiritual human are contained within us somewhere. I have passed through Six Thresholds in my life each with corresponding questions that I have had to answer, not in the sense of complete truth, but more as a realization that some questions cannot be answered just by science and philosophy and psychology but by simple resignation that the Mystery of Faith is beyond me, yet contained within me waiting for discovery. It is the place no one wants to look.

As a Lay Cistercian, hopefully, one grounded in the hope that God is the center of all reality and not me, I asked the question, "What are the six questions that are core to finding meaning in life?" Several years ago, I came up with what I termed thresholds of life, based on stages which I found myself passing through. That book I entitled, The Six Thresholds of Life. Since retiring, and having little to do to keep busy and stay out of the way of my wife, I turned to write down my thoughts. I consider these questions the foundations of spirituality.

What follows is my attempts to get as close as I can to answer what is meaningful. In a way, I actually failed because all I did was to make it possible for you to discuss these six questions with answers unique to each of you. That is as close as I think I can get without tripping over all my biases. To help me, I used Cistercian spirituality, a unique way of looking at reality that I find most consistent with being both human and an adopted son of the Father.

HOW TO USE THIS BOOK
Some books are designed for information and controversy. This is one which stresses contemplation and introspection in the silence of your heart. It is a journaling retreat. There are reflections and comments for each of the sections followed by opportunities for you to write down your thoughts. A further step, in this document, is sharing what you

wrote in a group of your choosing, e.g., in your parish. This is a book about Cistercian practices, specifically prayer, as I understand it. I am not a monk nor an expert in spirituality or theology. I am just a broken-down, old temple of the Holy Spirit, one in need of many daily prayers just to keep his head above the water of what the world teaches as meaningful. I distrust anyone who conveniently makes God the scapegoat for their failures in the lifelong struggle to answer these six, core questions of life. Some humans never do find the answers. My thinking is, you must ask the right questions to get right answers.

WHAT IS A LAY CISTERCIAN?

Since I put Lay Cistercian on the cover, I thought you might want to know what a Lay Cistercian is. This term is used for someone who follows the practices of Cistercian monks and nuns while not living in a monastery. www.trappist.net/lay-cistercian

I have freely chosen to be a Lay Cistercian and have been accepted by the Monastery of the Holy Spirit as someone who will try to love those around him or her with all their mind, their heart, and their strength. It is not as easy as it looks. I don't always succeed. What helps me is that the Monastery is a School of Love and Lay Cistercians are fortunate to learn some ways to adapt their conversion of life to live in the world.

A FEW OF MY ASSUMPTIONS

Anytime you read anything, whenever you hear a commentator on television news give an opinion, there are always assumptions underlying their thoughts. We can't help it. We speak of what we know based on our value system. Here are three assumptions I have about this contemplative practice of prayer.

ASSUMPTION ONE: We need to attend a school of love to learn how to love as Jesus loved us.

It would be foolish indeed to attempt to start my own school of Love when there has been one around since St. Benedict of Nursia wrote his Rule (c.540 A.D.) to develop rules to organize the monks of his day.

https://www.britannica.com/topic/Monte-Cassino.
http://www.osb.org/rb/text/rbejms1.html#pro
Notes:

Here is an excerpt from the Prologue of the Rule of St. Benedict.
> "LI S T E N carefully, my child,
> to your master's precepts,
> and incline the ear of your heart (Prov. 4:20).
> Receive willingly and carry out effectively
> your loving father's advice,
> that by the labor of obedience
> you may return to Him
> from whom you had departed by the sloth of disobedience.

*To you, therefore, my words are now addressed,
whoever you may be,
who are renouncing your own will
to do battle under the Lord Christ, the true King,
and are taking up the strong, bright weapons of obedience."*

He founded a monastery for monks at Monte Casino, Italy, which still follows this Rule. What is a school of love? It is a place where you learn the disciplines of how to love using proven practices and charisms (what you convert your life into when you say you want to be like Christ). The Christ Principle has endured to this very day.

These disciplines are not easily mastered and may take a lifetime of conversion of life only to realize they are beyond mastery, you may only approach them when you love others as Christ loved you. Each day is a lifetime in this school. Conversion is the curriculum. There is no graduation.

Cistercians (contemplative monks and nuns) and Carthusians (hermits) evolved from the Benedictine tradition c. 1090's, with a desire to love Christ even more fiercely. They did this through their contemplative prayers and practices (silence, solitude, work, prayer, and community), adapting the Rule of Benedict to each age. This is the same school that comes down to us today with the same practices, traditions, writings, wisdom, temptations, and graces in each age. It is a monastic tradition.

Characteristics of a School of Love
- *All Schools of Love have a Master.* The model, of course, is Christ whom we call *Rabonni* or teacher. He is the Master, and we are all disciples, in all ages, from all cultures and philosophies. The Lay Cistercians have a Master of their School, called an Abbot or Abbess. His person is the personification of Christ in the School. Humility and obedience to the command of Christ are paramount. "Prefer nothing to the love of Christ," says St. Benedict in his Chapter 4 of the Rule.

In the Church Universal, we have many religious orders of men, women, brothers, and laity. They all have a superior, one who represents Christ to the disciples.

- *The School of Love has a conversion of life as one of its purposes.* There is little value in a school that doesn't do anything to make you more than you were before. As a Lay Cistercian, I do not live within the walls of a monastery, but I do live within the walls of my own self. The more I make room for Christ in my life, the greater is my "capacitas dei" or capacity to love as Christ loved us.
- *A school is a discipline that helps me focus on love in the midst of a world full of Original Sin.*
- *The School of Love provides practices and charisms to enable you to touch the heart of Christ, who is the way, the truth, and, most certainly, the life.* Contemplation is a way to put you in the presence of Christ, then asks you to be silent in solitude to let God talk.
- *The School of Love stresses being present to the Holy Spirit in other community members.*
- *The School of Love begins the process of answering these six questions of life with Christ by using Cistercian spirituality and contemplation to provide meaning and clarification on what might seem murky.*
- *The School of Love approaches the Mystery of Faith in humility and obedience to the will of God, being open to the energy of the Holy Spirit.*
- *Each of the six questions must be answered in turn because they build on the answer before it.*
- *These six questions have not been fully answered but are in the process of being discovered.*
- *These are the six questions I had to discover. I use Cistercian spirituality in the form of Lectio Divina, Eucharist, Adoration before the Blessed Sacrament, daily Rosary, daily Liturgy of the Hours, and prayer to grow deeper into the Mystery of Faith.*

- *The School of Love bring joy to the heart, not the joy that the world gives, but the ability to love others as Christ loved us.*

We will spend the next three days together, part of your larger journey of life. It is what you do with the rest of your life after you go home that will sustain you for the rest of your life. It is time you take to overcome self-inflicted obstacles and temptations that say all of this is irrelevant and foolish and does no good, that is meaningful and makes the journey worthwhile. This journal-retreat is a trip to enter the one place no one wants to look, within you. If you allow, I will take you to a place where you may have never been, one that begins to answer the six questions the human heart asks. I will show you how contemplation and prayer using both mind and heart can unlock the darkness. Mystery continues to mean something beyond our mortal intellectual capability, but it will be welcomed as an old friend and not as a block to the truth.

If you wish to explore this topic more thoroughly, look up the following URLs.
- http://www.ben.edu/center-for-mission-and-identity/resources/rule-of-st-benedict.cfm
- https://thecenterforcontemplativepractice.org
- https://cistercianfamily.org/

Notes:

ASSUMPTION TWO: My contemplation follows the Cistercian Way. Cistercian (Trappist) spirituality with its unique practices of silence, solitude, pray, work, and community forms the basis of charisms (humility, obedience to the will of God, hospitality, simplicity, and Lectio Divina) that lead to the conversion of self to God. Lay Cistercians, following Cistercian spirituality, adapt the disciplines of the Monastery (without actually living there) to whatever their vocations might be. Contemplation is certainly not limited to one religious order, i.e., Cistercians, but it is the one which I use in all my books.

ASSUMPTION THREE: The Mystery of Faith is approached in at least five levels of spiritual awareness, each one leading to more deeper penetration of God's plan of action for us. I will use the transformative Word of God as an example of growing deeper in faith, love, and service.
- *Level One; Hear the Word with your mind*
- *Level Two: Pray the Word in your heart*
- *Level Three: Share the Word with others*
- *Level Four: Be the Word you hear, pray, and share*
- *Level Five: Enjoy the Word. Allow the Word made flesh to sit next to you in silence and solitude.*

(You will notice the same levels of transformation are also below.)

ASSUMPTION FOUR: Contemplation allows us to move from the realm of the mind to the realm of the heart. Contemplative spirituality is all about being silent, being in solitude, practicing Lectio Divina daily, sharing Eucharist daily, reciting the Liturgy of the Word together daily, converting your life to the Lift of Christ daily. All of these practices begin with the realm of the mind but develop into the realm of the heart. This realm of the heart is what we all aspire to attain.

As a Lay Cistercian, I reach this level of love and then slip back into my old self again. This notion of dying to the old self and rising to new self is core to the conversion of life into the Life of Christ Jesus. My purpose in life, as you will soon see, is based on Philippians 2:5. My life becomes trying and trying, over and over, to have in me the mind of Christ Jesus as a way I address these six questions of life. The journey is the important part of my attempts to love, sometimes even achieving fleeting completion, This is the deepest part of me, unexplored, like the darkness of a cave; unknown, yet luring me ever forward, like a moth seeks a flame.

ASSUMPTION FIVE: Dedication to a contemplative way of life is all about dying to self and rising again with Christ. Conversion of life is a lifetime process of striving to move from my false self to the true self, giving up the self of arrogance, pride, vanity and the allure of world to choose death, not life…Forever. The late Dom Andre Louf, the abbot of Sainte-Marie-du-Mont in Bailleul, France, wrote a book which opened my spiritual eyes and ears entitled, <u>The Cistercian Way</u>.
- https://www.amazon.com/Books-Andre-Louf/s?ie=UTF8&page=1&rh=n%3A283155%2Cp_27%3AAndre%20Louf
- https://www.amazon.com/School-Love-Cistercian-Holiness-Rhythm/dp/1853113433

The Cistercian Way is all about moving from the false self to God (true self) and how to use proven practices to seek God within you.

ASSUMPTION SIX: These six questions must be asked by each person, be they a disciple or an atheist. It is the answers that may be radically different for believers in Christ and those who are not. I actually wrote a book entitled <u>Spirituality for Atheists, Agnostics and Pagans</u>, in which I used these very same six questions without answers based on God. It is a great way to live a secular humanist life.

Lay Cistercians use Cistercian principles and practices of conversion of life, but do not use the Monastery as their occasion to express it. Here are a few of my obseservations about the differences betwthe een monastery and living the Cistercian Way in the world.

Early monks went into the desert to find solitude and silence in the wilderness. Ironically, Lay Cistercians find a wilderness of ideas and false self in the world, a place devoid of nourishment unless you put it there, a place with no water to quench the longing in the soul for Christ. The Garden of Eden is still the Garden of Eden because what God made is good. The majestic beauty of the physical universe, the natural law of all life, the wonders of science that delve into the very make up of matter and time with energy, all creation praises the Lord. The Psalmist writes in Psalm 148. *"Praise him sun and moon, praise him, shining stars, praise him highest heaves and the waters above the heavens,"* How can sun and moon praise God? They do not live, as we do? The Psalmist points to a very important reflectin about life itself. *When Sun and Moon be what they are destined to be, they automatically praise God be just being.* All life is like that, with the exception of humans. Humans don't act their nature, they tend to act like animals or not as their nature intended. Remember, Genesis 2-3 speak of a fall from grace? Adam and Eve were kicked out of the Garden of Eden (did not act according to how they were created) and had to suffer pain, death, and other human dysfunctions. Christ came to redeem us (restore us to be able to act our nature, except for the effects of Original Sin).

Matter and time are not evil, yet they will end. Humans are not evil, but all will die. While we humans live, we are tempted by the wilderness of false ideas, like Adam and Eve were in the story of salvation. We will be tempted to make ourselves gods until we die, yet, because Christ became one of us and paid the price for our redemption, rising from the dead to be our mediator with the Father once more, we have found adoption as sons and daughters. This is the Good News Christ wants everyone to know, even if they don't believe in Him.

In recognition of that great series of events (Philippians 2:5,-12) we proclaim the death of the Lord until He comes again in glory, using Cistercian practices and conversion of life. Lay Cistercians pray as they can, not with schedules of prayer but by transforming the very struggle and distractions into a hymn to the wonders of God's love for each of us. As The little fox tells the Little Prince, in Saint Exupere's tale of the meaning of love, it *is the time you take to discover the meaning of love that is itself part of loving.*

Lay Cistercians embrace time, not just as part of the make-up of the physical universe, along with matter and energy, but as an instrument to transform us from where we are now to where we want to be with our true self, one rooted in the Life of Christ in the best sense of that phrase. Time becomes transformative when both monks, nuns, laity all see themselves in relationship to the totality of all that is and proclaim, *Abba, Father.* Time exists to help us approach the Mystery of Faith in the now, so that we can live that same Mystery forever with the source of all energy, the pure energy of God in the Trinity. We all live in the context of time, but we do not all realize that we alone can transform ourselves from our false self to our true self by Cistercian practices and charisms into our intended nature in the Garden of Eden. Christ gave us, adopted sons and daughters, the power, not only to go to heaven, but to transform earth by recognizing that God is, God and we are who we are, then giving praise, as found in Revelation 4:11; *"You are worthy, our Lord and God, to receive glory and honor and power, for you created all things, and by your will they existed and were created."*

Of the many excellent, transformative ways to move from self to God that the Church has developed over the centuries (Franciscan, Dominican, Carmelite, Augustinian, Ignatian, Cistercian, Benedictine) I have chosen the Cistercian Way as my personal vehicle because it stresses silence and solitude in the context of Lectio Divina, Liturgy of the Hours, Eucharist, Adoration before the Blessed Sacrament and being what I read in Chapter 4 of the Rule of St. Benedict. Everything is geared to move from self to God.

Praise be to the Father, and to the Son, and to the Holy Spirit, now and forever. The God who is, who was, and who is to come at the end of the ages. Amen and Amen. –Cistercian doxology

FOUR WAYS TO HELP YOU APPROACH THE SIX QUESTIONS ALL HUMANS MUST ANSWER BEFORE THEY DIE

To approach a Mystery of Faith, a sign of contradiction in the physical and mental universes, and which is all there is in the realm of spirituality, God provides with you four gifts. If you remember the myth of Perseus, you know that he was Zeus' son, a demi-god. When faced with what seemed like an impossible task to kill the Kraken, Zeus helped him by giving him three gifts, a helmet (invisibility), a bronze shield (protection in order to kill Medusa) and a sword (power). Perseus used these tools to defeat his adversaries. Zeus did not fight his battles for him, but gave Perseus the tools to do it himself. It makes sense to think that God would not give us the reality we could not comprehend without also giving us the tools to be able to at least get a glimpse of what is on the other side of the foggy window. Saint Paul uses the metaphor of similar gifts to prepare disciples against the devil's tactics and to arm them for battle. Ephesisns 6:10-17. God leaves us free to fight the battle ourselves, but gives us tools and armor to help us. I call these perspectives, because you must use them to make sense out of these six questions. Together, they form four gifts to make sense out of what might seem non-sensical. They are:

- The Mystery of Faith: the one place Stephen Hawking could not look.
- How to enter at the place no one wants to look
- The Five Levels of Spiritual Awareness (again)
- The Two Realms of Prayer: the purpose of contemplation and conversion of self to God.

1. THE MYSTERY OF FAITH: THE ONE PLACE IN REALITY WHERE STEPHEN HAWKING COULD NOT LOOK.

Blog: https://thecenterforcontemplativepractice.org What follows is a blog I wrote on the death of Stephen Hawking as a tribute to his intellectual inquiry and insights he gave us about all reality.

MY REFLECTIONS

One blustery, blue day, as I sat contemplating Philippians 2:5, as part of my Lectio Divina, I looked out my office window only to see that the weather outside was foggy, so much so that I had second thoughts about going to Mass that morning. My thoughts, went to the late Stephen Hawking, grateful for his penetrating, cosmological insights into physical reality. I also thought of how, with all his brilliance and insights into physical reality, he could have missed the clues and signs telling of a deeper reality, one that we cannot see and measure with the tools of Science, at least so far. My thoughts swung radically to my own struggles with such overpowering phenomena such as divine energy, pure love, and pure knowledge. (Knowledge, Love, and Service for those who don't recall their catechism.) Then it all came together. The fog outside was like a veil, one clouding reality but not changing it, making it difficult to see clearly. Stephen Hawking, for all his insights, like so many of his colleagues who see reality through the lenses of just the physical universe, can't look at reality as it really is. Reality is clouded in fog, which I will label The Mystery of Faith, for lack of something more penetrating. It is like the dark matter and energy of the physical universe: you think it is there but have yet to prove it. Like Darwin and other apologists of only a procrustian, scientific approach to reality, Stephen Hawking just didn't see the bigger picture and how it all fit together. https://www.youtube.com/watch?v=bJVBQefNXIw

My next question was, why can the least in the Kingdom of Heaven recognize that there is a part of reality that is just beyond knowing and part of it hidden while the learned doctors of physics and medicine fail to comprehend it? Why is there just enough of it given to us to discern the meaning of love? Why did someone on the other side of the window (see the photo above) have to tell us what was on the other side and not to worry? Humans are not capable of fully knowing what awaits us as we fulfill our destiny in a place, not of this earth, the Kingdom of Heaven. To help out our senses and our limited ability to deal with the unknowable, God sent His only Son to show us how to live. With the Resurrection of Christ, the Kingdom of Heaven on earth began. We were welcomed as adopted sons and daughter of a loving Father, one that loved the world so much (John 3:16) that he sacrificed His only Son on the altar of the world, much like Abraham was willing to do with his son, Issac. (Genesis 22). Does this prove that God exists using the language of mathematics, physics, or chemistry? Probably not. It does prove that science can't look into directly at the Mystery of Life and make sense of what they find. They find it too ambiguous, too subjective, too much like a magic trick performed by Penn and Teller.

And then there is that fog outside my window, thick, impenetrable with my eyes, yet I know that something is out there, just like the photo above. I know that there is a physical universe out there, a rocky ball of gases following the laws of nature. I know that there is a universe where only humans live, although we are part of the physical universe. This is the universe of making sense of the physical universe of what was and asking what makes it up and how is it composed. It allows us to know that we know. Know what? One thing is how to access the ultimate level of reality, the spiritual universe, the Kingdom of Heaven (both on earth now, and in Heaven in the future). The third universe is one approached only by the heart using what we know with our minds. Faith informed by reason. Some will never be able to look at this universe and will see only the fog. Others will know there is something on the other side because someone from the other side came to us to show us how to see with the eyes that penetrate that fog of invisibility. The problem with invisibility is, you can't see it. Invisible reality is something science has a difficult time wrapping its theories around, yet it is the product of the greatest mathematical formula of all time, the product of three universes all moving together in one way, with one truth, and one life… Forever. This is pure energy.

As a Lay Cistercian, I have a big problem with a one or two universe hypothesis. Having tasted and seen the sweetness of the Lord, having experienced love beyond what this world offers, with its secular lures and false promises of gods, I know that there is something out there. Remember, the word "know" is not meant as the world gives it, but with humility and obedience to God's will, and a recognition that someone has given me the ability to see in the fog, even though my human senses fail sometimes. We discover that we are on this rocky ball of gases for a reason. Once we look at the universe, we ask, where is everybody? We have evolved human reason for a reason, i.e., to move to the universe of meaning. Like science, which just looks a the physical universe and seeks to discover the wonders of reality, so too does the mental universe allow some of us to approach the more radical view of reality, one that involves both visible and invisible reality, reality that is our destiny as humans, one that contradicts everything we know about science, but one that, if accepted, leads to life…Forever. This is not a barren rocky world human can inhabit, but the fulfillment of our human nature with help from the divine nature. With science alone, none of this makes sense, I agree. But viewing reality as a mystery of Faith, not the fog, but the reality some of which we can see and much of it which we can't, it makes some sense. Stephen Hawking looked at reality but just saw the fog. He did not use the tools of contemplation to look into the fog. Science has a theory for the big picture of matter, energy, and time, relativity. There is a theory for the small picture, quantum mechanics. What has not been explored enough is the spiritual solution to both using contemplation. Some of the answers to reality are contained within us. The six questions below are an attempt to frame some approaches to the totality of reality.

http://ccc.usccb.org/flipbooks/catechism/files/assets/basic-html/page-VI.html

For all his brilliance, the least in the Kingdom of Heaven is greater than Stephen Hawking. (Luke 7:29) He could not look at the Mystery of Faith, that there is a realm beyond knowing with our limited human intelligence, without seeing the fog. To be sure all those who espouse a spiritual view of reality may have faulty assumptions.

The early Church is replete with false prophets who claim they know the truth. We call that heresy, or faulty assumptions about who God is. One thing about all heresies is true, you have to have something against which they protest or want to change. I call that the Mystery of Faith.

We have a reason for a reason, to be able to discern not only what satisfies the mind but also what stimulates the heart to love in ways we still can't imagine, With his immense knowledge of physical reality, I hope he is enjoying the reality in Heaven that he so brilliantly explored on earth.

Just as the Church cannot be whole until both realms of the mind and heart are one, so too, science will never be able to see past or accept the fog of the Mystery of Faith with the tools that they have. My tools as a Lay Cistercian are the Rule of Benedict, Chapter 4. They enable me to move beyond physical reality with the "capacitas dei," capacity for God. To do that takes work and takes assumptions that are foreign to most scientists, i.e., the Resurrection, the Eucharist, that a being of pure love could love us. (Phil 2:5-12) Scientists are fixated on how humans can travel off of this planet to another habitable planet (which we have not yet discovered), rather than seeing this lifetime as training for how to live…Forever in a condition without matter, energy or time, based on the word of a Carpenter who died as a criminal. Crazy? Here is what's crazy:

- God made himself one of us to enable us to be in a different universe (spiritual) forever. How crazy is that?
- He gave us the tools for inter-universe travel. When approaching the Mystery of Faith, all these tools, all these Lay Cistercian practices and charisms don't sweep away the fog, but they do allow us to be even more convinced that there is something out there beyond my knowing so that we can continue to be convinced that we are on the right pathway. The great St. Thomas Aquinas, OP, when recovering from one of his deep contemplations, was asked if was healthy, responded that all I

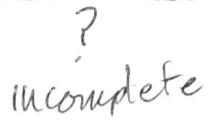

have learned about God up to this point has been so much straw compared to what it actually is.

- He provided us the atmosphere to survive this trip and to live, not on some planet we have yet to discover, but with him in a universe of love.
- He founded a school of love or charity to show us how to treat one another in this life and in the next. This school prepares us to live…Forever. How crazy is that!
- He rose from the dead to allow us to be adopted sons and daughters and heirs of the Kingdom of Heaven (for lack of a better term).
- He showed us the meaning of love by paying the ultimate price, dying on a cross, not from his wounds, but voluntarily giving up his life to the Father.
- He told us to love those who hate us, do good to those who scoff at us and speak all manner of evil against us.
- He said that the meek, not warriors inherit the Kingdom of Heaven, proving that the meek are not weak.
- He only left us one command: love one another as I have loved you.
- He made it possible to approach pure energy (the Father) through Him (Jesus), with Him, and in Him, to give glory to the Father in union with the Holy Spirit (the Advocate).
- He knew we were imperfect, like Adam and Eve (wanting toa a be god, saying one thing and doing another) but gave us the means to make all things new over and over again. (Penance, Reparation, Forgiveness, Change of Life).
- He knew our hearts would be restless until they rested in him. (St. Augustine)
- He told us to eat his flesh and drink his blood (the Lamb of God) to have life eternal.
- He said he was the Resurrection and the Life and that anyone who died and who believed in Him would never die.

- We have not even found any signs of life outside of this earth, much less sentient life. What if we are alone in the universe?
- We are not built to travel in space within the physical and mental universes. We have limited knowledge of the implications of weightlessness and prolonged isolation in space.
- Do you Wonder if we are not built for space travel but made to live out our time on earty? Why would that be? What are the implications of that line of thinking?

Some think Jesus was just a magician, some think he is not God but just a young man who had a messiah complex, some think his believers, after he died, covered up his real death and spread the story he rose from the death to quench their own ego for being correct, some won't see anything when they look at the fog rolling in over the lowlands, much less be intrigued by a blustery day in March. To those who do not see the assumptions and signs, be they scientists, movie stars who believe their own press, politicians who pander to the weak minds of those wanting another messiah, to false prophets who preach what they do not belive and believe they are the only one to whom God listens and through whom God speaks, to teachers of College-level Scripture courses who have lost the ability to know, to love, and to serve and to believe what they teach, to college students who are seduced by the lure of the fun-loving secular gods and goddesses and lose their direction, Remember, what you sow, you shall reap. I hope that God is merciful to you. Even more, I hope God is merciful to me, a broken-down, old temple of the Holy Spirit, one trying to make sense out of what God is trying to tell us through approaching the Mystery of Faith

THE MYSTERY OF FAITH

While trying to wrap my limited brain around figuring the out mystery, I came to this conclusion. I am wasting my time trying to know that which is beyond knowing, but still real. I have been asking the wrong question all along. .I thought clearing up the Mystery of Faith is an intellectual exercise by simply asking what is is, how it is, and why it is. It is beyond my knowing simply because what is there just is, like the photograph of the cup above, it is foggy and not able to be penetrated fully using any of the languages we know (mathematics, physics, chemistry, medicine, logic, or existential phenomenology). The language is the unscientific language of love, sacrifice, emptying of self for others, and dying to self to become more like God. That is not precisely the realm of the mind, but it is the realm of the heart. ~~It is the place~~ Stephen Hawking could not look at this place, not because he wasn't brilliant enough, but because his mind and his heart did not agree that the Mystery of Faith contained the answers to the human longing for fulfillment. To approach the Mystery of Faith you must open not only your mind but also your heart to Christ. ~~He~~ [Stephen Hawking], like many other humans, have not learned the dynamics of Mystery, the paradox that the more mysterious something is, the more real it is. Read the Cloud of the Unknowing. Warning: it is not for the faint of heart.

- https://www.americamagazine.org/content/all-things/reading-spiritual-classic-cloud-unknowing
- http://www.ccel.org/ccel/anonymous2/cloud/mp3

Notes:

Note: Ark

Jewish Scriptures say that no one can touch the Arc of the Covenant and live. The Arc of the Covenant was carried by special handles, so that no one would touch the Arc. Anyone who did, would die. The Holy of Holies is where God lives and only the High Priest can enter it. In the Eastern traditions of the thinking, mysticism, the Mystery of Faith is accepted as part of reality, the deepest part. In the Western traditions of critical thinking, influenced by Rationalism and Scientific Inquiry, the more we know something, the more it is real. There is quite a difference between the two *East and West*, evident in the dichotomy between pure science and pure theology. In the arena in which I live, contemplative spirituality using Cistercian practices and charisms, I accept the Mystery of Faith as a way to describe what is most real in the physical, mental and spiritual universes. That fact that faith is mysterious and doesn't fit the assumptions of science doesn't bother me. I choose the Mystery of Faith because it cultiates and leads us to the realm of the heart, where we can become what we believe and not just talk about it.

But Remember Aristotle v. Plato

In the Eastern tradition, the more mystery reality is, the more it is real. It is acceptable to be somewhat in the dark about the deepest parts of what is real. Like looking at a boat on a lake with early morning fog. Someone told you a boat is there and on the, way but you can't see it yet.

In the western tradition, W (see p.22) we want to discect it, see it, smell it, taste it, know it completely, pick it apart, control it for our own purposes.

THE PARABLE OF THE FOG
When straining to try to make the Mystery of Faith fit into my limited life experiences, I thought of an example that might make sense. What I saw was a boat on a lake sailing in a gentle breeze. All the landmarks were there, the shoreline, the sun rising, the compass that showed true North. Then, a strange thing happened. A fog appeared all of a sudden. Now there were no familiar landmarks. We still had a North on the compass, but there was a certain panic attached to the fog because we could not see where we were going, like the pilot of a plane flying solely on instruments.

Christ is the North on our compass. The fog is the limited ways we have to be aware of most of the reality (physical, mental and spiritual universes) which we can't see. Like an iceberg, most of reality is hidden from view, much like dark matter and dark energy, only this is white energy, the energy of love. Christ became human to show us how to steer our boat so that we have a way to reach our port, the Kingdom of Heaven both on earth and in Heaven.

I think of the great St. Thomas Aquinas who told people, towards the end of his life, that everything he had learned about God was so much straw, compared to what is actually out there.

Like Perseus' attempt to kill Medeusa, we can't look directly at Medusa without being turned into stone, figuratively speaking. Perseus had to use Zeus' shield of polished brass to look indirectly at Medeusa in order to cut off her head. God gives us the ability to approach the Mystery of Faith (everything in God's playground) with Christ as the shield, the sword, and the helmet of invisibility rolled into one.

Christ told us about Mysteries of God and adds "Don't be afraid." He says, "Trust me! The reason I had to come down to earth from the Heavens is to *show* you how to keep your eyes on me and learn of me, for I am meek and humble of heart. I could tell you about Mysteries, but your limited brain cells would fry from the overload. Just do one thing. Love one another as I have loved you, but do that in the presence of my Church, my Body, so you don't go off the deep end. Do what I do. Don't make love harder than it is. Life is simple. Humans make it difficult.

LEARNING POINTS

- The two universe hypothesis (physical and mental) deals with matter and time that is finite, even if some say they are infinite.
- The Mystery of Faith deals with the three universe hypothesis (physical, mental and spiritual) and is genuinely infinite, with time and space being finite. The mystery is reality but is just beyond our knowing, and just beyond our ability to uncover it with our minds alone, and just beyond what makes sense, yet it is real.
- The Mystery of Faith is real but faintly knowable. The Mystery of Faith comes from God to us in the form of faith, both faith of the individual and faith of the Church Universal. The Mystery of Faith enables us, through knowledge and love to produce something in the world (service), to be gardeners of all that is, to transform what is around us by converting our lives to that of Christ.
- The Mystery of Faith does not make sense to those who cannot look at invisible reality and use its power and energy to convert self to God.
- Stephen Hawking taught me to look beyond what I can see to find reality. I have reason and the ability to see how all things fit together so that I can approach reality as a Mystery of Faith.

- Science and philosophical thought combined, good as they are, are not able to look at these six questions and provide answers that are sustainable in both visible and invisible reality. Science does an excellent job of explaining why the pyhysical universe exists, how it exists and how it came to be. They don't do well with invisible reality, which asks the question why it is, and provides the only resonable solution to the Mystery of Faith. Not all spiritual outlooks give a plausible explanation to the Mystery of Faith. For the most part, they are rooted in themselves and practice relativism. "In ethics, the belief that nothing is objectively right or wrong and that the definition of right or wrong depends on the prevailing view of a particular individual, culture, or historical period."

YOUR REFLECTION

Look up the various definitions of relativism in the following URLs.
When you look out at reality, how does the concept of relativism, which I think is the base philosophy for most humans today, fit in with the notion of Mystery of Faith, seen as the great Cloud of the Unknowing?
http://www.dictionary.com/browse/ethical-relativism
Notes:

Can science and modern philosophy ever look at Mystery of Faith, given the history of the New Testament, New Testament and writings of the heritage of the Church, and fit them together?

2. HOW CAN YOU ENTER THE PLACE NO ONE WANTS TO LOOK AND FIND ANSWERS THERE?

There is a way to enter into your inner self, one that uses contemplation to approach the one source that has all the answers, that is the question, that shows you how to find fulfillment in the choas of the world. I will share with you what I have discovered about how to enter this dark cave and how to find the light of enlightenment there so that I can see the totality of reality, not just with my eyes but with the deeper recesses of my inner self. To do that I have to do several things, one of which is to build up the capacity for God within me. I have to make room for Christ in me, much like a surgeon uses extenders beneath the skin to allow the it to expand..

Prayer is the way, the door through which Lay Cistercians enter and approach the realm of the Sacred. This can be through realizing the presence of the Holy Spirit in the community, the School of Love, as St. Benedict was fond of saying. But there is a contemplative dimension to being part of a community of like-minded believers, if that makes sense. Contemplative here means moving from your false self to your true self. Christ tells us to die to that false self which the world seeks to establish in your heart in order to rise to a new life, one that is not of this world, one based on sitting next to the heart of Christ, one that is sustained by the energy of Christ Himself in God. Lectio Divina is one of the doors through which I enter into my deeper self to be present to what God has to tell me. I do that in the context of the of community because it is combining all the other Lectio Divina experiences of the Community of Love that surround me with the Holy Spirit and reinforces my own awareness of the Sacred. I would like to share what I have learned from the Lay Cistercians and monks of Our Lady of the Holy Spirit Monastery (Trappist) about how to enter the holy of holies of my heart and open it up to the heart of Christ through contempation. There are three steps or exercises that I will lead you through in the next pages. These steps are necessary tools to help you in Lectio Divina and to gain a capacity to see, to know, to do love as Christ has loved us.

CONTMEPLATION: THE DOOR TO ACCESS YOUR INNER SELF
: To probe deeper into reality, I am going to ask you to answer three seemingly innocuous questions, all of which are the same but all may be monumentally different, depending on your response.

QUESTION ONE:
This question uses your mind to probe deep into the physical universe, a deep dive into the realm of the matter, time, and energy. Go to a place of solitude in your life. Look at this photo for five minutes. What do you see? In the space below, write down only that which you can see with your eyes. Don't editorialize. Don't go any deeper than what the photo displays.

WHAT DO YOU SEE?

_____
_____
_____
_____
_____
_____
_____

WHAT DO YOU SEE?

QUESTION TWO: This second question uses your mind with your senses to probe ever deeper into both physical and mental universes, the realm of the visible universe with the capbility to find meaning beyond matter. Go to a place of solitude in your life. When you look at this photo for ten minutes, what do you see? In the space below, write down that which you can see with your eyes, as you did in Question One, but now add these questions, "What does this photo mean to you, if this is a picture of your life? What is in the cup? Who or What does the cup represent? What is the significance of a cloudy window? How does this photo help you contemplate your inner self? How does your mind help you to see associations and probe questions about meaning that Question One does not address? What does this picture tell you about your life? Write your ideas down in the following space.

_____
_____
_____
_____
_____
_____

WHAT DO YOU SEE?

QUESTION THREE: This third question uses your mind to probe ever deeper into reality, the physical, the mental universes with the addition of the spiritual universe within, the realm of the heart. Remember, contemplative spirituality means you look for the meaning of life within God's Kingdom. Go to a place of solitude in your life. When you look at this photo for fifteen minutes, what do you see? This third photo is the same as the other three but with a difference. Look at this question not only with your mind but also focus sitting next to Christ with your heart next to His heart. For Question One and Two, you have been asked to look ever deeper into your inner self. When you look at the photo now, what it is the cup you see? What you see now is God's playground and you are playing in it. How does this photo describe the Mystery of Faith, the meaning that reaches beyond physical and mental universes, embracing both visible and invisible realties?

_____
_____
_____
_____

Write down a sentence describing what you have discovered about how all reality fits together in one sentence. I know, it is impossible.

_____
_____
_____
_____

3. FIVE LEVELS OF SPIRITUAL AWARENESS

Almost every Sunday, except on my Lay Cistercian Gathering Day, the first Sunday of each month, you will find me at the 8:00 a.m. Eucharist, at Good Shepherd Community, Tallahassee, Florida. The Church floorplan is laid out like a fan. I sit in the very last bench in the middle, in the Handicapped section. Read Luke 18 and the story of the Tax Collector. I am the Tax Collector in my Church, an outcast, a broken-down old, temple of the Holy Spirit, someone forbidden to conduct a religious education class or lead a retreat or take a leadership role in the community, someone who cannot read Scriptures during Eucharist, someone forbidden to have a direct ministry and someone who is a sinner. I only sit in the very back of Church in the Tax Collector's bench, where I dare not look up to Heaven and proclaim over and over, "Jesus, Son of David, have mercy on me, a sinner." That is enough for me. I write all these ideas down because the Holy Spirit is the water gushing through the garden hose of my life and I can't seem to turn it off.

The Parable of the Pharisee and the Tax Collector

> *"9 He also told this parable to some who trusted in themselves that they were righteous and regarded others with contempt: 10 Two men went up to the temple to pray, one a Pharisee and the other a tax collector. 11 The Pharisee, standing by himself, was praying thus, 'God, I thank you that I am not like other people: thieves, rogues, adulterers, or even like this tax collector. 12 I fast twice a week; I give a tenth of all my income.' 13 But the tax collector, standing far off, would not even look up to heaven, but was beating his breast and saying, 'God, be*

merciful to me, a sinner!' 14 I tell you, this man went down to his home justified rather than the other; for all who exalt themselves will be humbled, but all who humble themselves will be exalted."

I have noticed that sitting in the very last pew of Church has an advantage. You can see people who come to Eucharist who do so because it is like the Elks or Moose Clubs. You can tell who pays attention or not. (I don't pay attention to the readings or homily all the time, either)

One of the big temptations is not to start judging the motivation of others by their outward demeanor. You can judge those inside the Church as to leading an immoral life but let God those outside the Church, says St. Paul in I Corinthians 5:13. As a Lay Cistercian, aspiring to move from self to God, I notice in myself five levels of spiritual awareness. All are based on the Word (John 1:1 ff). These apply only to those inside the Church, God judges those outside the Church.

LEVEL ONE: SAY THE WORD — At Eucharist, Liturgy of the Hours, Rosary, listening to the Scripture read at Holy Mass, and reading Scripture, I read the word. Remember the Word is God's word, not your's. It alone can cause a transformation of your Spirit. This is a level where we are distracted by cell phones, looking at what other people are wearing, making judgments in our minds as to who is holy or not. If you don't banish these temptations, it is difficult to move to the next level. It takes work to focus on Christ. This is the Church of the Mind,

LEVEL TWO: PRAY THE WORD – If you hear the Word and do nothing about it, you are like an orange tree that can't bear oranges. This level is one where you hear the Word of God and pray it. Prayer is the realm of the Heart. You go from your mind to your heart in most Cistercian practices and charisms. Praying in its purest form is lifting the heart and mind to God. Praying the Word is taking that Word, an idea, a sentence or a word and using it to link your heart to the heart of Christ. Only you can do that, but you can't do it without Christ. In the context of community, where two or more are gathered in my name, our Lord tells us, he is there. Remember, it is not how much you read Scripture or how many Hail Marys you say, although that is certainly Level One, it is what you do with the Word to make it flesh in your world. The temptation is to think that prayer won't do any good, or that all you have to do is ask God for favors and your needs and He must answer you. God knows what we need and He does answer our prayers but not in the way we might expect or in the timeframe we try to impose on God. This is the Church of the Heart. You play in God's playground now. If you want to use the sandbox, you must know the rules, love God through prayer, and serve others as Christ loved us.

LEVEL THREE: SHARE THE WORD –Growing ever deeper, you hear the Word, Pray the Word, but in the context of others, or the Body of Christ, the Church. This level realizes that the living Body of Christ, particularly the level of your assembly or local community of faith, has other who share their Word with you. There is only one Word. There is only one Lord. When you link up with the Church, you are open to the Holy Spirit coming down on you with the gifts you need to survive in this world, one that does not recognize Christ, one that wants to be God, just like Adam and Eve did. This is the Church of the Mind AND the Church of the Heart, the openness to the Holy Spirit. You will know this level when you reach it. This is the Christ who appears to those on the road to Emmaus and revealed himself to them in the breaking of the bread. The disciples related in Luke 24:32, "Did not our hearts burn within us as he talked to us on the road and explained the Scriptures to us?"This is the level where you have discovered the pearl of great price and are willing to sell what you have to possess it. Each of us must discover the purpose of our life, what makes sense of all the chaos. My purpose is Philippians 2:5,"Have in you the mind of Christ Jesus." That is it. It is the spoke in my wheel, the way in which I, as a Lay Cistercian, will practice loving God with all my heart, and mind, and strength and my neighbor as myself. (Deuteronomy 6 and Matthew 22:37).

LEVEL FOUR: BE THE WORD — The purpose of a monk, and therefore for Lay Cistercians, according to one of our Junior instructors, is trying to change from the old self to the new self, one who recognizes God as Father. The status quo or just maintaining yourself in spiritual awareness is not acceptable. The monks have a fancy word for it, *"capacitas dei"* or making room for Christ in your heart.

- This is the level of both the mind and the heart where you stand before the Throne of the Lamb in contemplation and wait.
- It is the level where you seek to make all things new by changing from self to God.
- It is the result of trying to have the Cistercian charisms of humility and obedience in your heart, without prescribing the results.
- It is the level where you just exist and don't have to prove anything to God, ask anything from God, dictate how God approaches you in your silence and solitude.
- It is seeking nothing more to life than to have in you the mind of Christ Jesus (Phil 2:5). That is it. It seeks first the kingdom of Heaven with the assurance that all else will be given to you.
- This is the level of transformation to Christ. It is not at all about you; all you do is put yourself on a park bench in the middle of Winter and hope that Christ comes your way.
- It is the level where you have heard the Word, prayed that the Word be done in your according to God's will, opened yourself to what the Holy Spirit directs you to be by listening to other Lay Cistercians and others who are marked with the sign of Faith in Baptism.
- This level is the product of all that has gone before.

- It is being open to the <u>ontic</u> possibility of the manifestibility of all being you encounter, in people, in nature, in animals and plants, in time and matter and energy.
- It is a balloon which you blow up to make room for Christ using the tools St. Benedict sets forth in Chapter 4 of the Holy Rule.
- It is the realization that, because of the pull of the world and the Devil, we are tempted to make ourselves into our own image and likeness instead of allowing God to be God.
- It is accepting the effects of Original Sin that we must suffer pain, earn what we get with the sweat of our brow, and eventually die, with hope in the Resurrection.
- This is the level that sets you up to enter the Mystery of Faith, to sit on a snowy park bench in the middle of Winter and be content to wait in silence and solitude until Christ should pass by.
- Science, worldly behaviors, those who do not see the Mystery of Faith with the eyes that go beyond physical and mental reality, those who see spirituality as so much history, like Napoleon, Daniel Boone, Davy Crockett, and President John F. Kennedy, can't live on this level. Reality is only what you can see and measure. This is the measurement of level four that you love one another as I have loved you.

The Pinnacle

LEVEL FIVE: ENJOY THE WORD — This is the level on earth where Christ actually sits down next to you on the park bench. He does not have to sit there. Your heart races with adrenaline, your senses are all peaking at the same time. You are flushed with a happiness you have never experienced for more than a nanno-second before this. You do not speak to Christ, there are no words needed, God's language is silence and solitude. You don't have to worry about what Christ looks like, no images or thoughts are adequate. This is a feeling, at the deepest level of who you think you are as a human. It is the fulfillment of Adam and Eve in the Garden of Eden, it is the living Resurrection sitting next to you. I must admit that I have only experienced up to Level Four and perhaps only a glimmer of Level Five. What I experienced was peace beyond all telling, and hope beyond my expectations. St. Paul says we see through a glass darkly, but then we will see face to face. My hope is this. I don't care about anything I have learned about the purpose of life as compared with knowing Christ. With St. Paul, I say:

> *"More than that, I regard everything as loss because of the surpassing value of knowing Christ Jesus my Lord. For his sake, I have suffered the loss of all things, and I regard them as rubbish, so that I may gain Christ."Philippians 3:8*

The product of the five levels of awareness are realizing the seven gifts of the Holy Spirit in your heart and possessing the fruits in your heart.. Like any product, they are meant to be lived, not read. What is different with this level is that it is not just for a second, it lasts for as long as you are in it. Joy is the ultimate product of any contact with Christ. John 15:11 states: *"I have said these things to you so that my joy may be in you, and that your joy may be complete."*

Heaven is a Mystery of Faith, a state of being where you live what you discovered while you are on earth that is authentic love. It is living the Seven Gifts of the Holy Spirit to the extent that humans can possibly do so, 100% of our nature, the maximum potential for our minds and our hearts, with Christ as the nuclear fusion (100% of His Nature) to fuel our joy. Christ is the mediator between human and divne nature, otherwise, we would have no chance to approach the Mystery of Faith. St. Augustine says that our hearts are restless until they rest in Christ.

THE FRUITS OF THE HOLY SPIRIT

When you sit on that park bench and are in the presence of God, you become what you sit next to, since this is God. You are not God, but assimilate the fruits of the Holy Spirit in your heart. You cannot *not* be a better person as you move from self to God, not by anything you did, but because Christ loves you and, hopefully, your fruits are that you love one another as Christ has loved you.

Galatians 5 states it most susinctly,

"22 By contrast, the fruit of the Spirit is love, joy, peace, patience, kindness, generosity, faithfulness, 23 gentleness, and self-control. There is no law against such things."

Note below the seven gifts the Holy Spirit spelled out below and write down your thoughts.
http://en.wikipedia.org/wiki/Seven_gifts_of_the_Holy_Spirit

LIST OF GIFTS OF THE HOLY SPIRIT

"The seven gifts are enumerated in Isaiah 11:2-3 and conform to the Latin Vulgate, which takes the list from the Septuagint. According to the Catechism of the Catholic Church] and descriptions outlined by St. Thomas Aquinas in the *Summa Theologica*, the seven gifts are as follows:

• *Wisdom:* Also, the gift of wisdom, we see God at work in our lives and in the world. For the wise person, the wonders of nature, historical events, and the ups and downs of our lives take on a deeper meaning. The matters of judgment about the truth, and being able to see the whole image of God. We see God as our Father and other people with dignity. Lastly being able to see God in everyone and everything everywhere.

• *Understanding:* In understanding, we comprehend how we need to live as a follower of Christ. A person with understanding is not confused by all the conflicting messages in our culture about the right way to live. The gift of understanding perfects a person's speculative reason in the apprehension of truth. It is the gift whereby self-evident principles are known, Aquinas writes.

• *Counsel (Right Judgment):* With the gift of counsel/right judgment, we know the difference between right and wrong, and we choose to do what is right. A person with right judgment avoids sin and lives out the values taught by Jesus. The gift of truth that allows the person to respond prudently, and happily to believe our Christ the Lord

- *Fortitude (Courage):* With the gift of fortitude/courage, we overcome our fear and are willing to take risks as a follower of Jesus Christ. A person with courage is willing to stand up for what is right in the sight of God, even if it means accepting rejection, verbal abuse, or even physical harm and death. The gift of courage allows people the firmness of mind that is required both in doing good and in enduring evil, especially with regard to goods or evils that are difficult, just like Joan of Arc did.

- *Knowledge:* With the gift of knowledge, we understand the meaning of God. The gift of knowledge is more than an accumulation of facts.

- *Piety (Reverence):* With the gift of reverence, sometimes called piety, we have a deep sense of respect for God and the church. A person with reverence recognizes our total reliance on God and comes before God with humility, trust, and love. Piety is the gift whereby, at the Holy Spirit's instigation, we pay worship and duty to God as our Father, Aquinas writes.

- *Fear of the Lord (Wonder and Awe):* With the gift of fear of the Lord we are aware of the glory and majesty of God. A person with wonder and awe knows that God is the perfection of all we desire: perfect knowledge, perfect goodness, perfect power, and perfect love. This gift is described by Aquinas as a fear of separating oneself from God. He describes the gift as a "filial fear," like a child's fear of offending his father, rather than a "servile fear," that is, a fear of punishment. Also known as knowing God is all powerful. Fear of the Lord is the beginning of wisdom (Prov 1:7) because it puts our mindset in its correct location with respect to God: we are the finite, dependent creatures, and He is the infinite, all-powerful Creator.

Comparisons and correspondences
St. Thomas Aquinas says that four of these gifts (wisdom, understanding, knowledge, and counsel) direct the intellect, while the other three gifts (fortitude, piety, and fear of the Lord) direct the will toward God.

In some respects, the gifts are similar to the virtues, but a key distinction is that the virtues operate under the impetus of human reason (prompted by grace), whereas the gifts operate under the impetus of the Holy Spirit; the former can be used when one wishes, but the latter operate only when the Holy Spirit wishes. In the case of Fortitude, the gift has, in Latin and English, the same name as a virtue, which it is related to but from which it must be distinguished."

Are these gifts of the Spirit and fruits that come from the Holy Spirit just empty musings of old men and women from the past, long dead and forgotten? Do these gifts exist today in your life? If not, how can you resurrect them through the Holy Spirit.?

Are these gifts of the Holy Spirit gifts that God gives us, similar but more effective than what Zeus is said to have given Perseus? How do these gifts from Christ help you to overcome the Kraken of life (Satan) and defeat the enemy, the false self within you?

4. THE TWO REALMS OF PRAYER: The purpose of contemplation is the conversion of self to God.

The fourth area for consideration has to do with prayer, one of the five Cistercian practices (silence, solitude, prayer, work, and community)

Contemplation is prayer in silence and solitude, seeking God in the depths of your heart. The purpose of prayer is to position you heart to sit next to the heart of Christ, then wait and listen to what transpires, as St. Benedict says in his Prologue, "listen with the ear of the heart."
Contemplative approach to prayer moves you from the head (knowing God with all your heart) to the heart (loving God with all your heart) so that you can love your neighbor as yourself. See Matthew 22:37-39 New Revised Standard Version Catholic Edition (NRSVCE) *"37 He said to him, 'You shall love the Lord your God with all your heart, and with all your on heart, and with all your mind.' 38 This is the greatest and first commandment. 39 And a second is like it: 'You shall love your neighbor as yourself.'"* This is how Christ wanted us to love one another, as He first loved us. It is the core of Jewish prayer, the **Shema Yisrael** of Deuteronomy, still practiced today and from which we take our purpose as the Church Universal.

As a Lay Cistercian, part of my growing awareness of the manifestibility of all being is due to my contmeplative prayer, consistently (daily) with humility and obedience living the Life of Christ as best I can.

Prayer, as I learned it back in Eighth Grade Catechism, is lifting the heart and mind to God. Nothing has changed over all those years since I sat in the Second Floor of St. Francis Xavier Grade School (the first public school in the state of Indiana) and heard the late Father Henry Doll tell us the purpose of life was to know, love, and serve God in this world and be happy with God in the next. (Baltimore Catechism, Question 6) Actually, everything has changed since I first heard about the purpose of life and how to pray. What is the same is that prayer is still lifting the heart and mind to God, but what is different is my growing ever deeper, imperceptively and ever so slowly, like the vast river streams at the bottom of the Pacific Ocean that take a thousand years to travel their route. What you can see, physical reality and mental reality is only the surface of something much deeper, elusive to the eyes and ears, but quite open to the heart of those who seek God with all their heart, and mind and strength and love their neighbor as themselves. (Matthew 22:37) This is the change, the growth in Christ Jesus, the song of the sirens of the heart to hear their cry and find peace in heart of Christ. St. Augustine said that our hearts are restless until they rest in Christ. <u>This fourth way</u>, the Cistercian Way, is contemplative prayer that move me from mind to heart, from self to God.

The end result of contemplation is the conversion of self to God. It is the fierce love for God in return for all that He has given us that compels us to be a sign of contradiction to the world. <u>Growing from self to God is moving deeper in your spirituality, filling the *"capacitas dei"* with God, making room for God in you and not your false self</u>. When you make room for God what fills the empty space? The gifts of the Holy Spirit, naturally. You just read about them above.

As a Lay Cistercian trying to follow Cistercian spirituality, I seek to transform myself each day into the Life of Christ using a contemplative approach to life. I do this by placing myself in situations that help me to focus more on Christ and less on me (Lectio Divina, Eucharist, Liturgy of the Hours, Rosary, Chapter 4 of St. Benedict's Rule, Contemplation before the Blessed Sacrament). I place myself in the presence of God and lift up my mind and heart and wait. I am never disappointed. Conversion does not mean I want to be God, like Adam and Eve did, but that I want to fulfill my destiny as an adopted son (or daughter).

This fourth way has to do with movement and growth, <u>both mind and heart, to become more like Christ and less like me</u>. I have found that a lazy attitude towards prayer will lead to my atrophying of any resolve to die to self. Spirituality, far from being easy, demands I take up my cross daily with all its temptations and struggle with the effects of Original Sin to win the prize, as St. Paul says.

One of the monks at the Monastery of the Holy Spirit, Brother Michael OSCO, asked us why monks and nuns give up everything to follow Christ? Isn't that absurd on the face of it? Having never quite thought this through, our group of Junior Lay Cistercians could not come up with a quick and ready answer. He said, "We give up everything so that we might grow and daily convert our hearts to Christ. That is what keeps us in the monastery." So, what does this growth look like? It might be more appropriate to ask, what does it feel like? This third way has to do with the conversion of the heart, and that conversion is based on allowing your heart to rest next to the heart of Christ. For me, this is another word for contemplation. Prayer has two dimensions, that of the mind and that of the heart. Most of us get trapped in the prayer of the mind, knowing about God, making the mistake of thinking that the more you know about Scriptures, the Church, saying many prayers in the hope of being more holy. The end result of prayer is always the prayer of the heart, or feeling the very beat of Christ's heart next to you. The Blessed Mother had this privilege and treasured all these things in her own heart. Reread the second tool above, the five levels of spiritual awareness. This example shows how we must grow deeper and deeper to reap the rewards of prayer. It is not enough to hear the Word, although that is good; it is not enough to pray the Word, although that is better; it is not enough to share the Word, although that is best. Beyond best is being the Word you hear, he Word you pray, the Word you share in your heart. This prepares our hearts to sit next to Christ on a park bench on a snowy day and wait for his presence, the Real Presence.

LEARNING POINTS
In a group of retreatants at the Monastery of the Holy Spirit, one of those attendees broke down and blurted out, I don't know how to love like you say. How do I do it? Where do I go?" Brother Cassian,

OSCO, said, "You learn how to love because Christ first loved you." This is a great learning lesson because it means our model, the template for love is how Christ loved us. How did Christ love us?

- As a Lay Cistercian, I find prayer has two dimensions, that of the mind and that of the heart. The realm of the mind has to do with knowing God with all our heart. The realm of the heart has to do with loving God with our hearts. The realm of the heart has to do with loving God with all our strength and our neighbor as ourself. (Deuteronmy 6 and Matthew 22:37).
- Praying means I voluntarily position my heart so that it can approach the heart of Christ. The transformation here is love, love from Christ to us. We know love because Christ has loved us first, first in Baptism with the Holy Spirit, then through the prayer of the Church Universal, diocesan community, and parish communities of faith. For me, I add the Lay Cistercian faith community to my list. Prayer is not a passive exercise. It takes human energy to access divine energy. I must proactively place my physical self in the presence of the Real Presence of Christ in Lectio Divina, Eucharist, Liturgy of the Hours, Rosary, reciting Chapter 4 of the Rule of Benedict every day, and then wait in silence and solitude.
- Praying means I seek to move from my mind (thinking about God) to my heart (becoming what I think about God.)
- Humility and obedience to what is in my heart are necessary for prayer. I have to keep reminding myself that I am not God and I am not the reason for prayer. The reason for prayer is to give glory to the Father through the Son and with the Holy Spirit.
- Prayer is lifting up my heart and mind to God. Lifting is such an important word here. I lift up the broken promises and failings of my life, all the times I tried to love God but I got in the way, all the times I say I love God but slide back into the brackish waters of Original Sin. All I can do is join what I have lifted up with what Christ lifted up on the cross and took with Him to present to the Father.

SIX QUESTIONS EACH OF US MUST ASK AND ANSWER BEFORE WE DIE

These six questions are core to what it means to me to be human. Even the fact that I can ask the question, much less give an answer that is consistent with all six, means I fulfill something not possible with a baboon or a salamander. Leaving aside the question of how humans developed reason, we find that we have reason for a reason. Why? Why do I have the ability to reason and animals do not? Yet, not all humans can agree with the results of their reasoning. Murder is committed because people don't agree. Wars are wages. Peoples enslaved. Kingdoms overthrew. Yet, we continue to ask the questions that shape who we are and where we are headed.

I am raising these questions because they are the ones I have had to answer, at least to my satisfaction, at this stage of my existence. These are questions I have had to struggle to answer, none of them answered completely, even now. These six questions are the foundation upon which any spirituity rests. It is the rock, the bedrock, the cornerstone of Cistercian spiritual practices. Before you seek God, these are some of the questions you must confront in the depths of your inner being. I submit that six of the questions facing humans are:
- What is the purpose of life?
- What is the purpose of my life within that purpose?
- What does reality look like?
- How does it all fit together?
- How do I love fiercely?
- I know I am going to die, now what?

QUESTION ONE: What is the purpose of life?
This is the first threshold through which I had to pass. I was about twenty-four or twenty-five years old, I can't remember which, when I asked the question for which I had no rote or glib answer. I contemplated on it for at least twenty years, even though I had formulated an answer. It is one of those answers that you think are just too simple to be true, so you use the crucible of time to test it six ways from Sunday to see what is true or not true. The purpose of life is why

we humans find ourselves as the only sentient beings, so far as we know, in the whole universe, much less the earth.

THE PURPOSE OF HAVING A PURPOSE
I asked the question once, what is the purpose of having a purpose? What I came up with was that it was a North on my compass, the North Star of my life, the reason why I am, the reason why I know that I know, and the grand design whereby all life has meaning. If you don't have a purpose for existing, a reason why you have reason, or a direction toward which all humanity is inexorably pulled, then you will find the remaining five questions irrelevant. Life will not make sense, even if it is sometimes confusing. You can ask the questons you want about the make up of stars, how far they are, how fast they are whirling away from us, and what is their composition. You won't ever find out the purpose of life.

Why are you even asking such an esoteric question, such as what is the purpose of life? Is there something in the human genome that causes us to wonder what is and what could be? Scientific inquiry asks questions about what is so that we might grow in the knowledge of who we are and find meaning for our and future generations. Art and poetry bring the human spirit beyond what is to ask what if something would be true, how would it look and feel. Baboons are not poets or write novels about war and peace. Of course, you might argue, how do you know that?

OUR SEARCH FOR MEANING
Ever since I read Viktor Frankl's book, <u>Man Search for Meaning</u>, I have been fascinated by our collective need to find meaning around us. Getting at that hidden, innate, yet real part of me that seeks something more in life than just a job, a family, a country club, a doctorate in Adult Education has been the focus in my later years. I have found a way to access that deep-vein coal tunnel running throughout my inner self. It is called contemplation and allows me to ponder on why, where, what, when, and who give me meaning and make life somewhat

reasonable. As one who aspires to be a Lay Cistercian, I go consciously into the mine shaft of my unconscious every day in an ancient practice called Lectio Divina. Google it and see what pops up. I only offer this for you to have a way to probe the richness and depths of your inner self. That is where you will find spirituality, that is, going within your spirit to discover new links of reality to each other, new ways of thinking about yourself and what you discover about what is meaningful for you. If you get nothing else from any of these ideas, I hope you would use contemplation as a way to grow deeper within yourself. The recesses of our inner-self are the one place we all fear to go. Why? We may have to face our demons or discover something that will change us in a way we don't anticipate, or just be in solitude with our naked self, stripped of all the vanities and faces we have put on to show others what we want them to see.Science may ask the appropriate questions for the physical and mental universes, but only the spiritual universe can answer the longing of the human heart. The answer is love, not the love that the world espouses (with you as god) but love that exists as energy, God's energy between Father, Son, and Holy Spirit. We would know none of this without Christ leaving the security of being God to take on our nature. Philippians 2:5-12.

WHY ARE WE ALONE IN OUR QUEST TO FIND PURPOSE
Have you ever noticed that Aardvarks don't have a choice about what is meaningful or not? What sounds silly might merit closer investigation. Think about it! All animals, indeed all living things we can observe, are born, they learn, they grow older, they procreate, they grow older, then they die. Only humans are the odd exception to the observable phenomena that all matter has a natural cycle of birth, existence, and death. Of course, we share all of the characteristics of matter with all other animals, but something is different. We have a reason, we have a choice, we can choose to endure pain for a greater good (apologies to B. F. Skinner). In observable reality, there is us, and then there is everything else. As far as we know, we humans are the only ones who ask What is the purpose of life? We can alter our future based on those insights. Is there a reason we have reason and others

don't? If we are the only ones who can ask our purpose, then what is it? That is why I think we are alone in our mental universe, just like I think we are alone in the universe.

LEARNING POINTS
- Life can go on without you knowing a purpose, but it sure makes it easier to find meaning which you know there is direction and purpose in nature and that life evolves into something for a reason.
- The purpose of life is to find out the reason why we have a reason.
- The purpose of life is to ask the question, When we look around at all that is, we see, hear, feel, taste, and touch what is meaningful and ask why? Monkeys don't ask why.
- Your meaning may be different than my meaning of life. What commonalities do we all share? The purpose of life is a personal choice you make to incorporate all your knowledge, all your experiences, and all your relationships into one statement that you use to justify what direction all life trending.
- Science does not ask the purpose of life question, so they do not have answers for it. What they do have answers for is, what is physical reality, what makes up physical reality.

YOUR REFLECTIONS
What is the difference between you and a baboon? Seriously! Think about what you have that a Baboon or any animal does not have. Why can you even ask about the purpose of life and animals just live the purpose of life but can't discover it like you? Write down what you think the purpose of life is? Remember, it is the purpose for all of us, not just you. Life means all being, all matter, all time, and all energy. You may have a favorite quote from Abraham Lincoln, or Cicero, or it may be a sentence from Shakespeare sums up why you find yourself alive today and part of a much bigger picture. If the purpose means life is worth living then you must write down what it is worth, what makes us unique in all the world, the reason for why we know that we know. Take some time and think about it. Write down your thoughts.

_____
_____
_____
_____
_____
_____
_____
_____
_____
_____
_____
_____
_____
_____
_____
_____
_____
_____
_____
_____

Think about what you wrote above, summarize purpose in one sentence or thought.

_____
_____
_____
_____
_____

GROUP ACTIVITY

Question One: What is the purpose of life?

EXERCISE:
In the space below, write down what you think the purpose of life is, all life. Take some silent time to reflect on this statement. You may wish to answer it with a sentence or two or even draw a diagram.

Draw diagram on this page.

This page is intentionally kept blank.

DIVIDE INTO GROUPS OF THREE:
Read these verses from Deuteronomy 6:4-7 out loud.
Read these verses from Matthew 22:34-40 out loud.

ANSWER THESE QUESTIONS:
1. How would you compare these two core centers of belief? Discuss how these two centers of Old Testament and New Testament are similar and how they differ. How does the New Testament improve upon the Old Testament and bring it to completion?

2. Can anyone really love with ALL their heart and mind? Why is this important for Cistercian spirituality? Compare diagrams you just drew above. What pops out at you from the comparion?

3. What is God's purpose for us? Read Deuteronomy 6 and Matthew 22:38 again.

As a group, be prepared to share two learning points from the discussion you just had.

REFLECTIONS TO CONSIDER:
- If the two Scripture passages from Deuteronomy and Matthew are indeed the core of our faith, and we accept them as such, then all our practices and prayers must ensure that we sustain that love through prayer. We stress contemplative prayer in this book, as practiced by Cistercian monks and nuns.
- It takes a lifetime of practice to love as Christ taught us, and even then, we will be perfect in this love only in Heaven, our final destiny.
- We do this most effectively by practicing how to love with others who have the same approach to life, i.e., the community of Catholic believers. We do this because practicing howtolove with those wholove us prepares us to confront the real challenge to belief,loving those who don't love you back.
- We need spiritual food for the journey (Eucharist) and the ability to start again and make all things new (Forgiveness).
- Jesus did not leave us gold, silver, or property as our inheritance. What he does is to give us exactly what we need to love with ALL or hearts and minds: Eucharist and

Forgiveness. He showed us how to love fiercely.
- By ourselves, we are unable to sustain this love with all our hearts and minds. We need God's grace and energy to help us keep our focus. It is only *in, with, and through Christ that we can give ALL glory and honor to the Father in the unity of the Holy Spirit*. --Doxology at the end of the Eucharistic Prayer.

QUESTION TWO: What is the purpose of my life?

Now that you have identified what the purpose of all life is, you must use this purpose to identify your individual purpose within that statement. Question Two identifies what you consider the center of *your* life, it is the one principle upon which all other values and assumptions stand. It is the keystone of your arch, the cornerstone of your building, that without which nothing meaning anything, the one center of your universe, as you view it.

You must choose your own center, just as I have chosen mine. It is neither good nor bad but the one principle upon which you use to measure all reality as you see it. Like everything else in life, there are false and true principles, and we can make poor choices. Animals don't have that ability.

I have developed a way that I select my one center that I want as the ground of my very being. Everything flows from my center. It is the one principle that, if I took it away, nothing would make sense. Resist the urge to think that there are two centers or more. That is just resistance at work where your mind wants to force you into relative thinking, that you don't need a center, that everything is a center.

BLOG ABOUT MY PERSONAL CENTER

What follows is a blog I wrote about my personal center from my site: https://thecenterforcontemplativepractice.org.

Everything has a center. The world. The universe. The galaxy. God. Christ. You. Of all of those, the one most elusive is YOU. Your center is the sum of who you are, the North on your compass, that one thing that, if you took it away, everything would be meaningless, or, put another way, nothing would make sense. For all humans, they choose to have a center. If you don't have one, life chooses one for you. In the New Testament, Christ put it this way: by your fruits, people will know you. Who you are is at the center of YOU. What you choose to place at your center is the one principle upon which all others exist.

In a game of darts, it is aiming for the bulls eye. Like all games, we have some natural talent to make the bulls eye or 100% but, for most of us, it just takes practice and practice. As one who aspires to be a Lay Cistercian, and who has promised to convert my life daily to living the life of Christ in me more and more, also called conversion of life, I have to practice to hit the bulls eye of life, but at least I know what it is. That I try and try to hit it is all I can do right now. Sometimes I do and sometimes I don't, but it is the trying that is my prayer, over and over, consistently, relentlessly, passionately. It is the pearl of great price, that certain something that I found that I would sell all I have to have it. It is like having a spouse that you love dearly, despite the inconsistencies of personalities and differences of what life is about. You give all to possess it, despite the rocky road you are on.

My personal center is one I chose about 1958. It was a conversion moment (we have constant conversion moments throughout our lifetime). I came up with this idea many years ago. It should not be confused with centering prayer, which it is not. It is the one principle that anchors your life, in my case, to the life of Christ. Without it, life ceases to have full meaning and I deteriorate to only having meaning that the world gives and not the unlimited depths of knowing, loving and serving that are the products of my contemplation. It completes my humanity in ways I could never have imagined five years ago. It sustains me through hatred, envy, jealousy, and the other temptations of the Devil (Galatians 5). It compels me to go places where I dare not look, inside myself. My center, one which I selected based on Faith (God's gift to me) is contained in Philippians 2:5. It is eight words long: *"have in you the mind of Christ Jesus."* That is it.

It is the only words (sacred words) that I have ever used as my Lectio Divina prayer. It is the reason I drive five miles (one way) each month to attend the Lay Cistercian Gathering Day with other fellow Lay Cistercians. It is the motivation for me to spend time each day in prayer, as much as I can, before the Blessed Sacrament and attend the Eucharist daily. It is my way to convert myself from my false self to my true self. It is what I hope to become eventually become now, and in Heaven. It is my center of everything.

THE RULE OF REVOLVING CENTERS
Like your tires, if you don't keep air in them, if you don't take them in when you get a nail in them, you won't be able to use them, a center needs maintenance. Some call it *conversio mores* (conversion of life). In terms of a tire, it is more air, and to stop the leaks, to keep the tires rotated and aligned. Your center is like an ice cube. It will melt if you don't keep it frozen. Like everything else in nature, the physical universe, it deteriorates. This is Orginal Sin, the archetypal stores of why we find ourselves in an imperfect state with death being the ultimate penalty.It takes work to keep your center aligned properly. Did you get that? No automatic getting on the conveyor belt of life. It takes work, your work. That is why, as a Lay Cietercian I must be diligent in taking up my cross daily to follow Christ. If not, my ice will begin to melt. My practice emcompasses the Cistercian Way, the spirituality that provides me with opportunities to place my heart next to the heart of Christ and know, love and serve as He loved us. By myself, I have neither the srrength nor the stamina to sustain myself agains the roaring lion who roams the world seeking whom he may devour. He devoured Adam and Eve, he could not devour Christ, and he most definately tries unrelentingly to keep me from practicing my spiritual exercises and charisms.

BE CAREFUL WHAT YOU CHOOSE AS YOUR CENTER
What you place at your center is God. That may cound corney, but it is true and the consequences, even if you think you are correct, can be life threatening (not your life in this world). There is such a thing as a false

center, just like there is a choice we have to be our false self or true self. Here are some false center I have considered but rejected.

Church -- the obvious selection for a center is the Church. Be careful. It is an eluring choice but one that is non sustaining. Church does not produce grace, but it is a conduit. Go for the source of power.

Blessed Virgin Mary-- In the window of the Abbey Church at the Monastery of Our Lady of the Holy Spirit, there are no pictures of saints or statues. In the back wall, there is only a stained glass window. Look at that sane photo of Mary below. What do you see? Nice colors? What else? Where is Jesus in relationship to Mary? Notice that Christ is her center, not the other way around. The Church honors Mary because of what she taught us: *do what he tells you.* Christ is always the center for Mary. Mary chose Christ as her center just as we have the opportunity to do. Mary tells us she is a poor center, but points us to a good one. My soul magnifies the Lord, she says. Take the next ten minutes and look at the photo, or better still, go into the Abbey Church and look at Mary. Just look.

Power—Power, in the sense that the world give us, is elusive and fleeting. We are tempted to make power our center when we think we are superior over others because of our money, our position, or economic advantages, our genetic breeding. True power comes from accepting adoption as a son or daughter of the Father, the source of all power.

Money-- Money may make the world go around, as Joel Grey sings in the musical, Cabaret, but it is a terrible center. People and nations kill others trying to possess it. Politics is about, not only power, but also money. It is like cotton cand, tt tastes good, but there is zero nourishment. Many religions are like that.

Fame-- Fame is fleeting. In fact, fame is the most disposable of all values. I watched I watched Bob Hope, Bing Crosby, Jimmy Stewart, President Ronald Regan all grow old and die. I still watch their movies. Fame is fleeting and makes a poor center, even if you have the Road pictures to keep you entertained.

Ego-- If you put yourself as your center, you have a fool for a god.
Hatred, Anger, Envy-- Placing hatred or envy at your center makes you do things that are harmful to yourself and humanity. The wrong center may seem like the right one for the time being (Nazi in WWII) but is innately corrupting of human values.

Family -- Your heart says your center should be your family. Centers are those values from which we derive our meaning for existence. Centers should be permanent. What happens to you is your spouse dies, your children die? What is your center now? Family is in my top four picks but not my center. My center is one where I will see my family again in the next phase of reality, living with God...Forever.

Scripture says to seek first the Kingdom of Heaven and all else will be give to you besides.

LEARNING POINTS

Here are some thoughts that have popped into my mind when meditating on my Center (have in you the mind of Christ Jesus) Phil 2:5

- What is God's center? Deuteronomy 6 and Matthew 22:38 and everything else that is
- What is Christ's center? To do the will of him who sent me and glorify the Father (John 17)
- What is Mary's Center? Christ 100%, 100% full of grace.
- What is the center of the Church? Christ is the head and we are the Body, the sign of contradiction

What are your thoughts and notes about these four centers?

Praise be to the Father and the Son and the Holy Spirit, now and forever. The God who is, who as, and who is to come at the end of the ages. Amen and Amen. --Cistercian doxology

HOW I SELECTED MY CENTER OF REALITY

STEP ONE. Take a regular sheet of 8.5" x 11" inch paper and divide it into four parts. Use scissors to cut them into four pieces. You should now have four pieces of blank paper in front of you. Line them up before you.

STEP TWO:
Option One: On the four pieces of paper in front of you, write down one idea on each of the four blank pieces of paper. They could be sayings, principles, ideas, values or thoughts that are the foundation of who you are. Use just one or two words or a short sentence to describe your foundational principles or building blocks of who you are. Take some time to think about what four values express your purpose in life.

Option Two: If you are up to the challenge, try this activity for Step Two instead of just writing down four ideas that come to your mind. Place yourself in a place of silence and solitude (no television, radio, third-party conversations). You have four blank pieces of paper in front of you on which you have yet to write anything. Before you write down anything, go back to what you wrote in The Purpose of All Life and look at that statement. Here comes the hard part. Look at this statement for ten minutes without interruption. Focus just on the words you wrote. Read them over and over and over for ten minutes. Avoid the temptation to think this is a waste of time. Remember, focus on these words for ten minutes. If you find this difficult to do, you are successful. It is difficult to focus on spiritual things more than ten seconds.. Your spiritual attention span (going inside you) is probably no greater than your intellectual attention span, about eight to ten seconds. Do what you can, not what you can't.

At the end of ten minutes, write down your thoughts on the four blank pieces of paper on the table before you.

STEP THREE: Now that you have in front of you four pieces of paper each with a core value, take away one of the four pieces before you, the one that is not a center for the others and move it away from the others. You should now have three pieces of paper in front of you. Yes, it is difficult to choose, which is why this is a deceptively simple exercise in preference, yet tricky, if you do it correctly.

STEP FOUR: Of the three pieces of paper in front of you, think about which one is the least important of the three. Which one could you live without, if you had to choose among the three? Move it to the side. If you have difficulty in choosing, you are successful. You now should have two remaining pieces of paper before you.

STEP FIVE: These two pieces of paper are the ones from which you must choose your center. Take some time and think about which one is dependent upon the other for support, which is the keystone of the remaining. Use this opportunity to change your mind about your choices and select new ones, if you have had second thoughts.

When you are ready, of the two remaining pieces of paper, select the one you think is your center, the core of your being, the one principle that, if you took it away, nothing else is the same. Move it to a place at the top of the four, with the other three underneath in a row. Now that you have a center, you need to determine if it is authentic and stand the stresses of time and meaning. Now what? The next step is for you to determine what all of this means.

ANALYZE YOUR CENTER: Is your Center authentic?

Here are three questions that I used to determine if my center would stand up to the wear and tear of life. Remember, this center is what I freely chose to be the North on my compass, my North star to guide me in my quest for the purpose of life in Question One. What is authentic is not what the world considers true. Christ is the way, the truth, and the life and all centers should be measured against the One who is.

> **Question One: How well does my center fit into the answer I used for the "Purpose of All Life" in Question One?** Everything in life or reality is linked together somehow. We may not have the ability to see how it is so or don't possess the technology to make that connection, but is all linked together as One.

Question Two: Is my center stable? Will I have the same center in fifty years? Seventy years from now? If not, why not. A center should be the core of who we are. We can add to it or discard what is not true, but the core remains true.

Question Three: Our center is the measure we use to determine what is meaningful for us. Now you know what it is important to have an authentic center. If your center is you, power, riches, fame, fortune and glory (Indiana Jones and the Temple of Doom), or things, you have a center that is not authentic, i.e., you are your own center. Adam and Eve had this center when they chose to be god. No one can have two masters, as Matthew writes in 6:24 (NRSVCE)

> *"No one can serve two masters; for a slave will either hate the one and love the other, or be devoted to the one and despise the other. You cannot serve God and wealth."*

YOUR REFLECTIONS
Why is having a center important for your contemplative spirituality?

_____
_____
_____
_____
_____
_____
_____
_____
_____
_____
_____
_____
_____
_____
_____
_____
_____
_____
_____
_____

LEARNING POINTS

- Everything that is, is bound together with meaning, in addition to relativity (big picture) and quantum mechanics (small picture).
- https://www.theguardian.com/news/2015/nov/04/relativity-quantum-mechanics-universe-physicists
- We may not know how it is linked together. The first two questions are those which only humans can ask and answer, at least as far as we know. Animals fulfill their purpose by living it out. Humans fulfill their purpose by living it out, but with a difference, Humans can choose a purpose for life that is not based on their nature.
- Our center is similar to the default on our computer. We always go back to it, unless we change the parameters of the settings.
- Each person, each one of us can choose a center for us. It could be a good one, a bad one, or none at all, in which case the default kicks in. The default is our animal nature.
- Setting our purpose in life does not mean we actually achieve it. If our purpose is to make lots of money and we fail to do that, the result will be we will not have lots of money. Selecting a purpose does not mean we will reach it, but merely aim at it.
- The center we select for our purpose in life informs our behavior and sets in motion values that guide us forward.
- If we select being married as our center, live that out for forty years, then our spouse dies, does that mean what we have selected a false one? True centers last until we die. They should not change, although we can change our center at any time if we think we have the wrong one.
-

YOUR REFLECTIONS

From the four pieces of paper from which you selected, look at the one that you have selected to be your center.. Put the other pieces aside for now. Look at your center. Look at the paper containing your center for five minutes. Let the thoughts come as they may. Ask yourself, if this is my center, what does that say about what is important in my life? If this really is my center, what am I doing daily to show that it is important. Write down your thoughts.

Based on what you wrote above, summarize your purpose in life with one sentence. I also found this difficult to do, but try it.

REFLECTIONS TO CONSIDER:
- Everyone has a center.
- Everyone can choose a center, one that has value and meaning for them.
- Not all centers are of equal.value. Their values is not relative, that is, everyone has values if they think they have value. Value does not depend upon the individual, but whether it is in keeping with purpose of ife.
- The purpose of life determines the authenticity of your purpose in life. Everything is linked to everything else that is.
- You are free to choose a center that will destroy you.
- Your center informs what your heart says. From the fullness of the heart, the mouth speaks.
- Authentic centers will provide a pathway to life…Forever.
- You must work to keep your center situated, lest it revolve.
- You can lose your center, if you don't sustain it daily.
- The first threshold should reinforce the second one, and so
- on.
- You are what you place at your center. If you don't feed your center, you end up with a dead one eventually.
- At the center of all reality is choice. Only humans have that opportunity. Where we get the principles to choose is the most important choice of all.
- We can fit into God's plan or God fits into our reality. Does the First Commandment have anything to do with how we choose what is good for us?
- Your center should not change, unless it grows deeper.
- Only God satisfies the hungry heart and mind.
- Because of the effects of original sin, all of us are pilgrims in a foreign land. Our true home becomes Heaven not this earth. What are the implications of such thinking?

QUESTION THREE: What does reality look like?

REVIEW
You should now have selected a purpose in life. Within that purpose of life, you should have identified one principle upon which all other principles are founded. It is called your foundation, your center, or the keystone of your life. You should have identified how this one principle is a core value for the others. It should stand up to the three measurements you use to determine if this center is authentic. If the purpose of your life is core to how you view reality, the next question is, what does that reality look like?

Having a view of reality should not be that difficult. What is, is, isn't it? It would be interesting to see how your view of reality compares with those of others, and what that means.

DO THIS EXERCISE IN PRIVATE
You will notice that this page is blank. Draw on this page what you think reality looks like? You may use circles, pictures, drawings, or relationships to accomplish this. This is an excise where you reflect on the question for four or five minutes. Don't write anything, use your mind as a *tabula rasa* (blank slate), then write or draw what comes to mind. Later, you will share your ideas with others and form one view of reality.

(This page is intentionally left blank for you to draw your ideas.)

ANSWER THESE QUESTIONS IN YOUR GROUP OF THREE:
Using the paper provided, discuss what your just drew or wrote to come up with ONE view of what reality looks like. Be prepared to explain any images, symbols, or assumptions you might have put on paper.Read the Reflections to Consider (below) to give you some thoughts.

REFLECTIONS TO CONSIDER:
• The first threshold should reinforce the second one, and so on.
• This threshold provides you with meaning to help sustain you as you struggle to keep yourself centered with God as the basis for your reality. The ability to make all things new again is key to taking up your cross daily and following the example of how to love as Christ loved us.
• Our bodies and minds need nourishment and meaning to grow and develop. What nourishes our spiritual self? • I have been born again 25,500 times as of today. I say that because each day I am bid to take up my cross and follow Christ. I don't just get on the faith conveyor belt and get off when I die. Life is a struggle of temptation between good
and evil (Galatians 5:16-26). Sometimes we win, often we fail. Without the grace that comes from adoption as a son or daughter of the Father, none of us would have a chance at Heaven.
• We are pilgrims in a foreign land, once we have been accepted as adopted sons and daughters of the Father. God helps to sustain us in our journey to…Forever. We receive God's own energy in the Eucharist, and practice forgiveness as Christ taught us. Recite the prayer, the Our Father, to see what I mean. This world is not our destiny. It is full of temptations and evil.
• Faith does not and cannot live in the vacuum of your spirit. It exists in a sinful world with others. If people share in The Spirit, this is called a faith community.
• Once Mary accepted the invitation from God to be the mother of His Son, time changed. The spiritual universe is at odds with the physical and mental universes. The poles reversed, as it were. Now, the sign of

contradiction is the norm. The lion lies down with the lamb, God becomes Man, the Virgin shall conceive and bear a son, the greatest among you must be the least, and the leader among you must serve everyone.

Notes:

QUESTION FOUR: How does it all fit together?

REVIEW

The answer to this question is linked inexorably to the first three answers you gave to previous questions. Take some time and review what you wrote for the purpose of life (general), your purpose of life (specific), and what reality looks like.

To be able to link everything together in a way that makes sense to you depends on your assumptions about how reality could all fit together in a unified whole. Take a few moments to write out your assumptions about reality. Reality does not change, but our perception of it does, base on our assumptions.

Let me give you an example. One of my assumptions is that there are three universes to reality (physical, mental and spiritual). What we mean by those three universes may differ depending on our assumptions. Spirituality may be something different for each person, or it may mean I accept principles peculiar to a way of thinking, such as Gnosticism or Democracy. For purposes of this book, I define spirituality the realm of the inner self, with values and meaning as defined by you and inspire by the Holy Spirit.

Once you have identified the purpose of your life, what your purpose in life is within that general purpose, and what reality looks like, you face the next question. What does it all mean? The human mind, what I have come to see as the mental universe, seeks to make sense out of all that is. Scientists seek answers to the human genome, astrophysicists want to know how everything works, poets want to describe love, loss, death and meaning in life.

DIVIDE INTO GROUPS OF THREES

ANSWER THESE QUESTIONS:

1. What are the measurements to discover physical and mental reality? Are there different measurement for what is visible and what is invisible?
2. Who determines what is true?

3. What are the measurements to discover spiritual reality? How can you measure the Mystery of Faith? Is it like Microsoft's Cloud?

4. If you live in just two universes, what does that look like? Why would that make a difference in the way you look at reality?

5. If you live in three universes, what does that look like? Why would that make a difference in the way you look at reality?

6. Is what is essential invisible to the eye? (St. Exupere, **The Little Prince.**) What is essential?

7. What importance is this statement in discovering a deep knowledge of reality?

8. What does it mean that all shall be one? Are we heading for oneness with the One? What does that mean?

Be prepared to share two learning points from the discussion you just had.

Notes:

REFLECTIONS TO CONSIDER:
- In my world-view, there are at least three distinct universes. The physical one is composed of matter, energy, time, and space. The mental universe provides us with the tools and language to explore the visible universe using mathematics, chemistry, physics and human reason to determine what is true. Poetry, literature, logic and psychology allow us to look at both visible and invisible reality, find meaning and what is true. The

spiritual universe looks at everything that is and identifies what is meaningful and true using principles from
- God, the source of all authentic truth.
- There is only one truth in all that is. Any knowledge of reality must take into account all three universes, the invisible as well as visible reality.
- If you just believe that all reality is only physical and mental, what does that do your purpose of life?
- Just a the mind allows us to find meaning in our living out what it means to be human, so too, the spiritual universe makes sense out of that human meaning, giving direction, a sense of finality into one reality and a sense of purpose to all that is real.
- Some people don't use God's laws as the basis of their morality or world view. How do you keep your value system intact in the midst of all these ideologies and theologies?

Notes:

QUESTION FIVE: What does it mean to love fiercely?

REVIEW

In my case, I was not able to address what love is without answering the four questions before this one. Love does not live in a room by itself. It is one of the products of the human mind in connection with the human heart. Of course, mind and heart are symbolic seats for knowledge and love. We can see love in others by how they act and their values, what they have discovered as meaningful in their lives. We can go inside ourselves to contemplate about love so that we can discover a meaning that is spiritual (contained in my spirit). Love is meant to be shared. Sharing that love can be in marriage, but also be between parents and children, family members, friends, and even acquaintances whom we don't even know. Love is part of the equation for the purpose of life as well as a core principle of the meaning of what it means to be human. To a great extent, our life is about seeking the love of self and love of neighbor and doing something to make it happen in the reality in which we find ourselves. Fierce love is the intensity of that search for meaning.

MY REFLECTION: WHAT IS LOVE?

One of the most elusive challenges to face humans is that of love. Along with the sexual drive, which we all share with all animals and plants, it is a mystery for many. A mystery, because we just think we know what it is and there is a deeper side to it we have never discovered. A mystery, because we think we can possess it and define it once and for all and we realize that we don't know that much about it at all. Poets and novelists print thousands of pieces dissecting and proving every orifice of love, yet they still struggle with possessing it in its entirety.

Eric Fromm, author of the book, <u>The Art of Loving</u>, has been someone that has influenced how I look at love. Here is a quote from the art of which he speaks.

> "The first step to take is to become aware that love is an art, just as living is an art; if we want to learn how to love we must proceed in the same way we have to proceed if we want to learn any other art, say music, painting, carpentry, or the art of medicine or engineering. What are the necessary steps in learning any art? The process of learning an art can be divided conveniently into two parts: one, the mastery of the theory; the other, the mastery of the practice. If I want to learn the art of medicine, I must first know the facts about the human body, and about various diseases. When I have all this theoretical knowledge, I am by no means competent in the art of medicine. I shall become a master in this art only after a great deal of practice until eventually the results of my theoretical knowledge and the results of my practice are blended into one — my intuition, the essence of the mastery of any art. But, aside from learning the theory and practice, there is a third factor necessary to becoming a master in any art — the mastery of the art must be a matter of ultimate concern; there must be nothing else in the world more important than the art. This holds true for music, for medicine, for carpentry — and for love. And, maybe, here lies the answer to the question of why people in our culture try so rarely to learn this art, in spite of their obvious failures: in spite of the deep-seated craving for love, almost everything else is considered to be more important than love: success, prestige, money, power — almost all our energy is used for the learning of how to achieve these aims, and almost none to learn the art of loving."

Love is not only knowing, which is most definitely is, it is also doing. Fromm states that: "Love isn't something natural. Rather it requires discipline, concentration, patience, faith, and the overcoming of narcissism. It isn't a feeling, it is a practice." In my short lifetime of trying, yet consistently failing, to love with all my mind and heart, I find this statement to be inspired. He also gives the requirements for authentic love. "The mature response to the problem of existence is love." "Is love an art? Then it requires knowledge and effort. Love is not a spontaneous feeling, a thing that you fall into, but is something that requires **thought, knowledge, care, giving, and respect** (my emphasis). And it is something that is rare and difficult to find in capitalism, which commodifies human activity. "

In this question about fierce love, the very reason we need to include love at all is to go to the heart of what it means to be human rather than an Anteater.

LOVE IS LIKE A VALENTINE CARD
Love has two dimensions, that of the mind (knowledge and logic) and that of the heart (emotion and feeling). Remember when you were in Third Grade and everyone exchanged Valentine Day cards? What did you do, when you went home that day? Did you put them in a special spot in your drawer where you could pull them out and look at them frequently? Did you think of the person who gave you the card with affection? Did you feel a sense of warmth and pleasure? Love is one of the ways humans are different from other living things. It is a form of communication between two persons, heart to heart, thinking of others, wanting to help others. It can be with two humans or groups of humans. It can be between single persons, homosexuals, heterosexuals, groups of peoples, with families and relatives. Love is a human phenomenon. Love does not exist between animals, or between and animals and humans, although we can love our pet. Animals can't love back. So, what is this love? It is one of the thresholds through which all of us must pass.

Mature love is so much more than a Valentine's Day card. Here are Eric Fromm's five criteria for authentic loving with some thoughts about both dimensions of the head and the heart.

THOUGHT
Love is thinking of the one you love all the time.
Love is having their picture on your desk and in your heart

KNOWLEDGE—
Love is wanting to know as much as you can about your love.
Love is wanting the one you love to know as much about you as possible.

CARE
Love is patient with the one you love as they explore life.
Love forgiving of others, realizing that you are not perfect.

GIVING
Love knows that your loved one likes A-1 sauce on their steak and you make sure you buy it at the store.
Love is learning the art of receiving from your loved one, allowing them to love you in return.

RESPECT
Respect is wanting your love to succeed and do what it takes to ensure they meet their goals in life.
Love is taking the time to tame your other, waiting for them to grow and mature.

If you say you love someone, but don't do anything to show it, there may not be love there at all but just your representation of what it means in your own mind. Similarly, if you receive Faith from God but hide it under s bushel basket and don't do anything with it, there may not be Faith there at all but just your representation that you have made yourself into God.

YOUR REFLECTIONS
Write your thoughts for each of Eric Fromm's five characteristics of authentic love.

90

THE DARK SIDE OF LOVE

There is a dark side to love. This is a delicate topic which can be misleading, if not put into its proper context. Fierce love is so great that it transcends loving those who love you back, propelling you to the higher meaning and deeper feeling. It is the glue that allows marriage to continue, even if you are legally married but mentally divorced. Divorce is so easy in our society that couples give up on a relationship when there is discord or heat. You may find this topic uncomfortable or even strongly disagree with the dark description It is my attempt to say love sometimes calls on us to give all we have, to empty ourselves completely without asking anything in return. If you don't like the term "dark" what would you call it. The important thing is "love" not "dark". Fierce love includes dark love.

Fierce love will go to extreme lengths to serve others and keep them safe. It is selfless love. It does not count the cost of how much sacrifice is used to help others. Fierce love, like a raging fire, won't go out in time of crisis nor abandonment, it will not leave others unprotected, even if it an animal or someone you do not even know.

EXAMPLES OF DARK LOVE.

- Dark love is like the marriage vow that says I will love you in good time and in bad, in sickness and in health, no matter how rich you are or how poor you may become.
- Dark love is the person who must give up everything to be with their partner or child, such as someone who has leukemia.
- Dark love is the person who has to give 90% in a relationship to the other person's 10%.
- Dark love is the mom and dad that sell all they have to keep their children healthy and off of drugs
- Dark love is the son who gives up his job to be able to feed and care for his mother with Alzheimer's disease.
- Dark love is someone who puts up with verbal abuse and terrible personal humiliations with someone who has Borderline

Personality Disorder or Anger Mood disorder without hating them or screaming back at them.

- Dark love is putting up with the hatred of children who accuse you of being in la-la land when you try to move from self to God. It loves your children, even when they seem to abandon God and the heritage you taught them.
- With dark love, love does not count the cost or the suffering you must endure to be with someone who needs you.
- With dark love comes living out the sign of contradiction, loving those who hate you, not returning evil for evil talk, and loving those who harm you. Dark love is not easy. It is sometimes putting up with a spouse or parent who has mental issues or alcoholism and doing something to help them, rather than divorce or abandonment.
- Dark love is telling people the truth they do not want to hear, not because you want to hurt them but to help them.
- Dark love is the price you pay to keep love intact, even if those around you discount you for your insensitivity.
- Dark love is loving those who hate you, be they spouse, family, or neighbors who live next to you.
- Dark love is not responding in kind to threats to your dignity, your motivations, to those who genuinely hate you and call you fat, stupid, a failure at whatever you have tried to do in life, smelly, never doing anything right, someone they hate.
- Dark love means you give up following your own path in life, the safe and comfortable one, the wealthy one, the one that has prestige and honors due it, the safe way to go, to follow that which is full of challenges and uncertainties, and one that may lead to your death or at least much anticipated suffering. Such persons do exist, and in greater number that we might expect.
- Dark love is the single mom who takes up the responsibility for raising their children, either because her spouse died, or abandoned her.

- Dark love is the school teacher who throws himself in front of a bullet, dying to save his students.
- Dark love is a soldier who died trying to save his unit or someone who gives his arms or legs so that others might keep theirs. What loves is more fierce than that someone gives up his life to save another.
- Dark love is giving my life for another, living my life to help others, devoting my life to focus on the love of Christ.
- Dark love is taking care of spouse or parents with dementia or Altzheimers.
- Dark love is staying in a marriage that is 90/10% sharing, caring and, relationship, with you being the 90%.
- Dark love is first helping others to follow their dream and purpose in life before you pursue your direction.
- Dark love is not discounting or degrading your spouse or your children when they disagree with you.

As one who aspires to be a Lay Cistercian, I view dark love as the price I must pay for the pearl of great price, the treasure I would sell all to possess, even though those closest to me don't have a clue what that means for me.

ANSWER THESE QUESTIONS:
1. Reread Threshold Two. How does this threshold help and sustain Threshold Two?
2. Examples of loving fiercely are all around us. What are some examples?
3. Can only humans love fiercely? Are we even capable of loving fiercely?
4. Did Adam and Eve love fiercely? Describe their relationship before and after the fall?
5. Why is Jesus called the second Adam? Read Romans 5:12-21.
6. Did Jesus love fiercely? What was his relationship with the Father and Holy Spirit? Can you have that same relationshipwithin you?

7. Humans get the energy to love fiercely from God's grace. What does that mean when we take the very life of God in us? How should we act?
8. How does a contemplative approach to spirituality unleash our ability to love fiercely?

Be prepared to share two learning points from the discussion you just had.

REFLECTIONS TO CONSIDER:
- The first threshold should reinforce the second one, and so
- on.
- Fierce love comes only by plugging into the energy of God. Service to others is the result of loving fiercely.
- Good works for the sake of good works only benefit you. Fierce love that comes from God benefits everyone and everything.
- The ability to make all things new again is the key to taking up your cross daily and following the example of how to love as Christ loved us.
- Read Phillipians 2:5-12. What does that tell you about fierce love?
- The word "fierce" refers to the intensity of love and the lengths you go to sustain it.
- Fierce love, like faith, can be lost by lack of use. A contemplative way of life that stresses silence, solitude, prayer, work, and community is one in which love can flourish fiercely.

LEARNING POINTS
1. What extent would you go to keep your relationship with others intact? What would you give up to help your friends who are in trouble, financially, perhaps hooked on drugs, or just losing their job?'
2. Would you give up your comforts, your world, as you know it, to live in a totally foreign world with which you are not familiar? Christ did. (Phil 2:5-12)

YOUR REFLECTIONS

How would you describe dark love in your own life and in the lives of those you know? Is dark love real or just a fantasy? To love fiercely is to love those who may not love you back at all. Why is this question so important for discovering your purpose in life? (Question Two) Write down your thoughts about dark love.

_____

Make a list of those things you see as dark love around you.

_____

THRESHOLD FIVE: **How can I love fiercely?**

GROUP EXERCISE:
For the next twenty minutes, in the silence and solitude of your heart, ask the Holy Spirit to be with you. Look at the photo of the bench and imagine youself sitting there waiting for Christ. No thoughts, no agenda, no prayers. Wait. Can you just sit there for ten minutes?

WAITING FOR THE MASTER
You are seated on a park bench in the dead of Winter. Jesus has told you He will be passing by the bench sometime soon. You seat yourself and look down the path, straining to see Christ as he comes around the bend of the trees. You don't know what he looks like, but you have an invitation to meet with him today, and all your senses are at their peak. You don't want to miss him.

The first person to come to the trees is an old woman pushing a cart full of what looks like bottles and rags. You smile as she passes and wishes her a good day. She turns back to you and asks if you have a bottle of water. She says she has not had water in two days. You only have half a bottle of water left, but you give it to her, asking her to excuse your germs. She trudges away, smiling.

You look up, and there is what looks like a teenager. He asks if he can sit on the bench with you. You do not know him and are reluctant to let him sit down but he has on only a thin T-shirt, and it is very cold outside. "Thanks," he says. He talks about how he is homeless, and the Shelter kicks them out at 7:00 a.m. and he has no place to go. Again, you look to the pathway straining to see if Christ is coming. No Christ. The teenager says he is twenty-seven years old and out of a job with no family and nowhere to go. You get out your cell phone and call the local Catholic Charities and speak to someone you know about helping the young man. You help out there once a month with packing food for the homeless, so you are familiar with their services. It happens that the City has a long-term shelter for people who need job skills and a safe place to stay until they get a job. You give him the directions to the shelter, about eight blocks away. He gives you a hug and trudges away. It is going on two hours now, and no Jesus. A dog comes up to you, a Weimaraner, tail wagging, happy to see you. "Hey girl," you say. "Where is your Master?" She sits down and offers you one of her paws to shake. Friendly dog, you think, but who could be its owner? It is going on three hours now, and it seems to be getting colder. Just you and the dog are there, which you have named Michele. Just as you wonder once more if you have been stood up and inconvenienced, an older man approaches. He has a long, gray beard, somewhat matted together and uses a cane to help him wobble down the path. His clothes are neat but certainly well worn. His face has a gnarly look about him as if he had weathered many hardships and they had taken their toll. He asked if he could sit down since he was tired. You say, "Of course, I am just waiting for a friend to come by here." "You look cold," he says. "Here, take this scarf that my mother knit for me, it will keep you warm." The dog sits next to the man as if he was it's owner. All the while he kept stroking the dogs head and petting it on the head. "Oh, by the way," the old man says "this is my dog. Thank you for finding it for me." Two more hours went by but you do not notice because the conversation is so warm and intimate. You tell the kind gentleman all about your trials and successes and how you just want to seek God wherever that might be and whoever it might be. The gentleman tells you that He has to go home to see his father, to whom he owes everything You think of how lucky the old man is to have such a loving Father. The old man gets up and smiles at you. "You are a good person," he says, "and I look forward to seeing you again in the future," his face just beaming with kindness. Turing to his dog, he says, "Coming?" The dog jumps up and down a few times, wagging his tail fiercely and they both set off trudging slowly away from the bench. You look at your clock and see that five hours have passed, but passed so quickly. You are a bit disappointed that Christ did not stop by. You think maybe you got the time wrong and leave to go home. As you are going, you remember you have on you the scarf which the old man gave you as a gift, knit by his mother. You are shocked by what you see. On the scarf is embroidered your name in the gold thread. You think to yourself, he said his mother made it for him. Another thing you noticed. You felt your heart burning within you as the old man talked to you on the bench. "I wonder," you think, "...I wonder." The only prayer you can think of comes into your mind. Praise to the Father and the Son and the Holy Spirit, now and forever. The God who is, who was, and who is to come at the end of the ages. Amen and Amen.

YOUR RESPONSE

Now, look at the photo of the park bench for a few minutes. Think about the story you just read while focused on the park bench. What thoughts does the Holy Spirit place in your mind? Write down what your heart tells you about the story you just read. How does this relate to where you are in your Lay Cistercian or another spiritual journey?

ANSWER THESE QUESTIONS:
1. Write down your thoughts about the bench meditation.
2. What does this story tell you about meeting Christ?

3. If you say you have never seen Christ, but can't see Him in your neighbor next to you, what do you need to change to be able to seek God?

Write down, in one sentence, what fierce love is.

REFLECTIONS TO CONSIDER:
- The first threshold should reinforce the second one, and so on.
- Fierce love comes only by plugging into the energy of God.
- Service to others is the result of loving fiercely.
- Good works for the sake of good works only benefit you. Giving someone a cup of water in the name of Christ is charity.
- Fierce love comes only from God and benefits everyone and everything.
- The ability to make all things new again is the key to taking up your cross daily and following the example of how to love as Christ loved us.
- Read Phillipians 2:5-12. What does that tell you about fierce love?
- The word "fierce" refers to the intensity of love and the lengths you go to sustain it.
- Fierce love, like faith, can be lost by lack of use.
- A contemplative way of life that stresses silence, solitude, prayer, work, and community is one in which love can flourish fiercely.
- Is fierce love the same as dark love?
- For those who have fierce love, the person in front of you is the most important person in the world, at this time.
- Fierce love is using 100% of one's nature. Humans can never reach it in this life. With Christ filling up in us that which we lack in love, we can use 100% of our nature (when we get to Heaven, not on earth).
- Fierce love exists in the realm of the Heart.
- Fierce love is Matthew 25:31-46.

Praise be to the Father and to the Son and to the Holy Spirit, now and forever. The God who is, who was, and who is to come at the end of the ages. Amen and Amen. –Cistercian doxology

QUESTION SIX: You know you are going to die, now what?

REVIEW

This last question for me is one of summation of my whole life. If I have answered the first five questions correctly, then my life is fulfilled, The big question is, am I correct? Who determines what is correct in your thinking? You do, not so? But you are going to die sooner or later. Then who determines what happens to your estate? Is there something more to life, something higher or deeper, towards which all humanity is propelled and compelled to be? Interesting thought as you make your final summation.

You have answered the question about what the purpose of all life is, and what your purpose is within that framework. You have identified, at least somewhat, what reality looks like. You have answered, or begun to answer, the question of how all reality fits together and what it means. Narrowing the answers, you have begun to identify what fierce love is and how it fits into the prior four questions.

The question sets forth and statement followed by a question. The statement is, you know you are going to die. Do you doubt you are going to die? What does your experience tell you? What doesn't die? The question is, now what do you do? Here is the context in which I had to answer Question Six.

I DIED ONCE ALREADY

I know I am going to die, I just don't know when. In 2007, I had cardiac arrest (The Widowmaker) and died in the Emergency Room. I am still here (although some debate this). In 2014, I was diagnosed with Leukemia (CLL type) and it is in remission. Other people I know have been diagnosed with various types of cancer. Some have survived, others have not. All of us are going to die. It is what happens between that wonderful window of birth to death that determines how each of us answers these six questions or thresholds of life.

We all face threats to our life and challenges to our way of life. My own diversions, both positive and negative, have been (in no order of time):

- Marriage,
- Daughter
- Lay Cistercians
- death in the family,
- Columbine,
- Sandy Hook,
- Hurricane Katrina,
- losing a job with Unysis
- Retirement from Department of Community Affairs, Florida
- Retirement from Department of Children and Families, Florida
- Retirement from Department of Vocational Rehabilitation, Florida
- Groundskeeper for George Rogers Clark Memorial in Vincennes, IN
- Masters degree from Loyola University
- received a Doctorate in Education,
- the present idiotic, political morass,
- Catholic Church denying me a membership for 17 years
- the rise of Islamic Fundamentalism or any ideology that seeks to suppress freedom of thought or activity
- Leukemia (CLL type)
- The Widowmaker (heart attack),
- The US. Army Chaplain
- Catholic Priest
- growing older over 77,
- having a meaningless job for most of my life.
- Parkland, Florida Shooting
- Member of a group that Prays the Liturgy of the Hours, twice daily
- Wrote 51 books that no one has read.
- (https://thecenterforcontemplativepractice.org)

My point is, life is what happens to you, some of which you control, other situations over which you have no control. It is what you do with all that noise, that stuff, that is the sum of who you are. Out of all that jumble of competing ideologies and "isms" we must make sense of it all. It is my responsibility, my choice that is important. These six questions all build on one another and are dependent on the one before it. They take a lifetime to discover, if ever at all. The purpose in life, my purpose in life, how I view reality, how I fit into reality, the meaning of fierce love, all exist to answer the last question, now what? I do know that I am going to die. I can't stop it. All I can do is make sense out of life using these three questions to know that I have not lived in vain, that there is the reason for a reason and I have used it to discover meaning. If my answer has been correct, I am fulfilled as a human being, a member of the collective consciousness of all the minds and hearts that have gone before me.

THE FINAL THREE QUESTIONS GOD WILL ASK ME

I have never been good at taking tests. I could never figure out why but I know that I learn differently from most folks. I look at the big picture and like to see how things fit together. There is a test that all of us must take, no exceptions. You can be atheist, agnostic, heretical Roman Catholic sect, member of the authentic Church Universal, non-Christian sect, scientist, philosopher, or Gnostic, and it does not matter. There are no exceptions. It is that time when you must stand before God and give an account of your stewardship. Can you pass God's test?

WARM UP EXERCISE

Here are a few warm-up exercises to get the brain cells synapting. You must look up the answers in the URL provided.

If the center of Christ is God (Father, Son, Holy Spirit) what is the center of the Catholic Church?
http://ccc.usccb.org/flipbooks/catechism/files/assets/basic-html/page-VI.html Deuteronomy 6 and Matthew 22:37.

Is belief the same as Faith? What is greater than Faith? Faith comes from God, belief comes from your will. I Corinthians 13:13.

Why were the Scriptures written? John 20:30-31.

THE BIG TEST

What three questions will God ask you to see if you got what He was trying to tell you through Christ? Of course, I don't know what the three will actually be, but I know the three that I am preparing for as I stand before my Father as His adopted son to give an accounting of my stewardship. Faith will not save me, if all I did in life was believe, because Faith is not the purpose of the Life of Christ, it is the engine, the power, the truth that leads to the purpose.

What is the purpose of Life? It is the *Shema Yisrael* found in Deuteronomy 6 in the Old Testament and fulfilled by Christ in the New Covenant in Matthew 22:37. God gives us the purpose of life as well as the means to fulfill our destiny as humans. Not everyone will see the answers to this question. What happens to those who missed the boat, whose train has left the station, who are caught naked in the bitter cold without a coat? Who will judge them? God will. I use a saying that helps me from becoming god. "You are not me, I am not you; God is not you, and you, most certainly, are not God." --mfc

What is the purpose of your life? Based on my trying to love God with my whole heart, my unique purpose is, *"have in you the mind of Christ Jesus."* (Phil 2:5). Being a Lay Cistercian helps me to focus on taking up my daily challenge to seek God. My helps are: Eucharist, Lectio Divina daily, daily reading of Chapter 4 of St. Benedict's Rule, Liturgy of the Hours, Rosary, Adoration Before the Blessed Sacrament as much as I can.

What did you do to love others as Christ loved you? An orange tree that does not bear fruit in Florida is cut down to make way for those who do. The proof of Faith is doing, not believing. You can't do unless you believe and love with all your heart. All the questions are linked to each other. Read Matthew 25:31-46.

Loving others as Christ loved you is the ultimate test of Faith, Hope and Love, and the greatest of these is Love. I am preparing for this test not only by what I know, but by what I do, which shapes who I am.

HERE IS A PITHY THOUGHT

Even if there is no God stuff, or Resurrected Jesus, or the Holy Spirit is just my misguided hope in eternal life, if I followed the Cistercian practices and charisms, I would, at minimum, be leading a life that enriches my humanity and fulfills my destiny. With God, with the Christ who rose from the dead and Ascended to the Father taking me with Him, with the Holy Spirit to guide me in my quest to seek God through Cistercian spirituality, I would be fulfilling my destiny in three universes (physical, mental, and spiritual) and inherit the Kiingdom of Heaven for which I was destined before there was physical energy and time.

Praise to the Father and the Son and the Holy Spirit, now and forever. The God who is, who was, and who is to come at the end of the ages. Amen and Amen. --Cistercian doxology.

YOUR REFLECTIONS: Does God judge you on your merits and stewardship? How does Matthew 25:31-46 fit into being a member of the living Body of Christ on earth? How does the community of the faithful help you to lead the Life of Christ? Does contemplation help you touch the heart of Christ and move from self to God?

_____
_____
_____
_____
_____

THE GRAND CONCLUSION THAT IS JUST THE PROLOG

Looking at the sentences you wrote for each of the previous five Questions, write down what your theory of everything is. Do this privately. Read the URL to get a flavor of what some are saying. Look up what Einstein had to say about a unified theory.

https://www.google.com/search?q=unified+theory&oq=unified+theory&aqs=chrome..69i57j69i65j0l4.3751j1j7&sourceid=chrome&ie=UTF-8

Looking at what you wrote for your one theory of all reality, what has your life been worth? What are your aspirations yet to be realized? List the challenges you have had in life. How did you resolve these dips in your life? Is your road rocky? Are you on the wrong road?

_____
_____
_____
_____
_____
_____
_____
_____

EXERCISE: Pair off into groups of threes. Count off by groups. For ten minutes, think about your group question by yourself and then, after you have writtn down notes, discuss them with your team mates.

ANSWER THESE QUESTIONS:

1. All of us are created to live forever with God. This is our destiny. We are pilgrims in a foreign land when we live in the spiritual universe while on earth. What must we do to let go of all false centers in order to empty ourselves of all that is of this world?

2. Based on what you have learned from the first five thresholds, how would you answer the questions posed by the sixth threshold, "You know you are going to die, now what?"

3. Read John 11:25-26. What does this mean to you as you face moving from this earth to be with God…Forever?

4. Why is hope in the resurrection so important to those waiting to mve to the next level of reality?

5. What do you plan to do with the rest of your life to ensure you reach your destiny in Heaven? Do you have another destiny?

Be prepared to share two learning points from the discussion you just had.

REFLECTIONS TO CONSIDER:
- The first threshold should reinforce the second one, and so on.
- If you have a void of meaning in your life, do everything you can to fill it. Just make sure the filling includes God.
- Be passionate about life and making a daily routine.
- If God has not been center to your life, you have a chance to make it so.
- In the end, all we have is Hope that the words of our Savior

are true. Remember Hope is upper case. What does that signify?
- See the mysterious and radiant force of God in everything around you; discover that God in your neighbor; love unconditionally with all your mind, your souls, your heart. If you have done this, you are already in Heaven. Personally, I still have a way to go.

MESSAGES FROM THE EDGE OF TIME

1. If Heaven is the reason why we are here on earth, why is it we don't do more to prepare ourselves to live there?
2. It is betterfor youto have the perspective that all humans have the opportunity to get to Heaven, than to think that only a few make it.
3. If you play around with worrying about who is going to Heaven, you risk playing god. That is against the first commandment.
4. You are goingto die, no matterif the doctor tells you, you have cancer, or you just die from old age.
5. All humans are destined for Heaven, but not everyone will make it there. Who goes and who does not?
6. Our Master came to SHOW us how to get to Heaven.
7. Everyone has a path in life. Just because your road is rocky, doesn't mean you are on the wrong road. Walk the path of your destiny.
8. In your life, there are four doors through which you must pass. Do you know what they are and what each means?
9. The Master is the Way, the Truth, and the Life. Do you know what this means in your life, right now?
10. No one goes to the Father except through the Son. How does this affect your relationship withGod? The purpose for The Master coming to earth was to glorify the Father. What is your purpose?
11. Do you have a pattern of spiritual behavior? Contemplative?
12. Who has the right to take their own life? What are the moral implications of suicide or assisted suicide?
13. How would you explain reality in terms of three universes?
14. What is the purpose of the spiritual universe?
15. The core values of life are those we discover on our own, but also those given us by The Master. What are they? What is the value of these core principles for those who know when they are going to die?
16. Have you made the self-directed retreat?

17. Why should you help others to refocus, when you are the one who is going to die? How can this be a golden opportunity for you to share your spiritual treasures with those whom you love?

18. Everyone has the right to live. Everyone has the right to die with dignity. Not everyone agrees on what that means.

19. Cremation is an acceptable form of burial. It is certainly less expensive. Go to www.saintmeinrad.edu, to access a place that sells wooden urns for cremation.

20. If it a good idea to have a lastwill and testament, it is also good to complete a journal preparing for the journey to...Forever.

21. Do you have a pattern of spiritual behavior? What you live on earth will be your frame of reference in Heaven. There is a caveat. Your experiences must be rooted in authentic, spiritual principles.

22. You based your life on God's core values. Do you know what they are? You measure yourself against God's core values to find out how close you are to being authentically human.

23. Look at the human race as heading towards its destiny. You, too, have personal destiny, Heaven.

24. The purpose of life is to know, love, and serve God in this world, so that you can be happy in the next level of reality.

25. What you know about the purpose of life and God's design is what you take with you to Heaven.

26. In the physical universe, you live, love, and die. In the mental universe, you broaden your horizon by loving through principles that lead to meaning. In the spiritual universe, you do all of the above, but use God's core values to actually boost you to a higher level of meaning. You prepare to live in a world without matter, a world of pure energy, pure thought, pure service, and pure love.

27. You need help to get to Heaven, even though you must enter there by yourself. Your spouse helps you, and so does your family and friends. Church is just a group of friends that are linked together as the body of The Master. You must enter through the one door, The Master.

28. Beliefs are those we hold with our minds. Faith is a gift of God we are given for our hearts. All beliefs have assumptions. Those

assumptions differentiate a Protestant from a Catholic, and Jew from a Muslim. You should be free to hold any belief system you choose, but know that all of them cannot be correct. They are in conflict with each other, in terms of the assumptions they hold to be true. All humans are destined to be with God in Heaven. Depending on your assumptions, you may believe that people must agree with yourinterpretation of history and the Scriptures to make it there. Remember, Heaven is God's playground, not yours. God is the ultimate judge of the heart.

29. To die well, you must also have lived well.

30. Preparing for your death, be it next week, or next fifty years will be the same process.

31. God takes care of those who believe in Him.

32. Soon, in about three or four billion years, the Sun will engulf this planet as it expands and expends it energy. By that time, the human race must find new worlds to pioneer and ways to get there. Will we? Who knows. There is a way we can make it off the planet right now. When you die, you move to a different universe. This universe contains pure energy, pure thought, pure love, and pure service. While you are on earth, you prepare forthe trip, the most important trip of yourlife. It is not a vacation nor is it business travel. Your destination is to live in God's home...Forever. How will you prepare?

33. You can't have hatred and love in the same room together. Hatred is a way of de-valuing people and yourself. It is not the same as not liking the personality of someone. Hatred means you wish them ill, you can't stand to be in their presence and you despise their key values.

34. We can hate people or we can hate ideas. If we hate ideas that are evil, as in the hatred of sin, we are justified. If we hate people, such as a spouse, we might be justified in our hatred, if that person is doing something evil and against God's law. Usually, we hate the sin but love the person.

Clearly, we must love one another, despite our failings, in spite of their personality flaws.

35. Marriage is a commitment of fierce love that overshadows our faults and gives obedience to God's thinking. Read Matthew 22:34.

36. Fierce love is love and forgiveness for those who hate you. Fierce love is the love God has for us. There is no place for sin or hatred in the presence of this kind of love. It is the most difficult to achieve because it contradicts our instincts—to hurt those who hurt us, to strike back at those who bad mouth us and call them name

37. Invisible reality or taking the word of someone is the most difficult part of Faith. Blessed are they who have not seen and yet believed.

38.

Write down any thought you might have that you would like to remember when you go home. Did any of these ideas trigger other thoughts in you?

___
___
___
___
___
___
___
___
___
___
___
___
___
___
___
___
___
___
___
___
___
___
___

List those dreams, places to visit, goals you would like to have happen before you die. Prioritize them. Don't put anything down unless you plan to do it.

WHAT DOES YOUR CONTEMPLATIVE PRACTICE LOOK LIKE?

HOW I DESIGNED A SYSTEM OF SPIRITUALITY TO SUSTAIN MY CONTEMPLATIVE PRACTICE

The following pages are samples of the horarium (hourly agenda) I use to organize my day as a Lay Cistercian. I must tell you that I am retired and have time to devote to the practice of how to love as Jesus did. Not everyone has the great opportunity I have, to pray the Liturgy of the Hours and Rosary in the parish. If I don't keep it, no big deal, but it is an anchor. I off you an example of what I have used to design a system of spiituality for my particular needs. Being a Lay Cistercian, when looking at a way to practice contemplative spirituality, I am mindful of the following characteristics:

- *Each day,* I must try to use it routinely as a habit. The practice of contemplative spirituality is just that, each day, at the same time, without fail, to do what you say you are going to do. I can look back on my week and examine my couscience to see how well I did. There is no sin attached to doing or not doing it. It is how much time and attention I give to sitting next to the heart of Jesus. If I am to deny myself and take up my cross daily and follow Christ, then I must daily practice the exercises that give me the srength to do that.
- *Each day*, I must pray as I can. The great advice from Brother Michael, O.C.S.O. is so simple yet so profound. I now pray as I can, when I can, where I can, and how long as I can.
- *Each day,* I must seek a balance between my prayer life and my work. My work, being retired, is to devote time to writing my blog and books that help parishes to use contemplative prayer as a way to move away from my false self closer to Christ.
- *Each day,* I try to increase the "capcitas dei" trying to make room for Christ. I do this by not watching hateful television news shows of all networks, or reading the Tabloid-obcessed major newpapers and magazines who spew hatred, falsehood, hopelessness, and secular values that make those, who are seduced by the siren call of making themselves into god.

My Center: Have in you the mind of Christ Jesus. –Philippians 2:5

Five or Six Practices to support my center: These are Cistercian charisms and practices.

1. Silence—When I think of silence, I think of lack of worldly noise.But, it is more than just lack of external noises, like television,children playing, going to work, and traveling in a car. For me, I tryto be conscious that all these sounds give glory to the Father throughthe Son, in union with the Holy Spirit. I try to make a space whereI can reflect on my center with some degree of privacy. Silence ofmy heart helps me sustain the other Cistercian charisms andpractices and so grow in fierce love.

2. Solitude--- Solitude, for me, means carving out a space and quiettime to focus on how to have in me the mind of Christ Jesus.For the Cistercian monks, solitude means carving out a time and space that permits them to focus on loving God with their whole heart, whole soul and whole mind without external distractions. For the Lay Cistercian, we also concentrate on fashioning a little prayer nest but we live in the secular world and therefore embrace all the distractions as part of our prayer to the Father. St. Benedict says, "That in all things, God be glorified."

3. Prayer—Prayer is lifting the heart and mind to God. As a Lay Cistercian, I actively put myself in the presence of God using prayer, both public and private. Even if I sometimes feel that prayer is repetitious and rote, I have noticed that the more I try to grow deeper using prayer, rather than fighting the externals, the more peace there is in my spirit. It is resting my heart in the heart of Christ that helps me love fiercely.

4. Work—Work as the world sees it is a means to make money. Work with a spiritual approach is transforming the ordinary tasks of the day into those that give glory and praise to the Father. Work is prayer, if offered up as praise and glory to the Father.

5. Community—Lay Cistercians gravitate towards communal gatherings to refresh the soul and to transform themselves deeper in the mind and heart of Christ Jesus. Even though there is great distance between us, we link together as one in our commitment to each other because we are all linked through the mind and heart of Christ Jesus. Sharing Christ with each other nourishes the Spirit in me.

My spiritual goals for the rest of my life:
1. Take up your cross daily and follow Christ. The cross in this case is being consistent in spiritual practices. Although there is no penalty attached for not preforming them, the more you want to have in you the mind of Christ Jesus, the more you will have what you wish for. Take what comes your way and transform it through Christ Jesus.

2. Solitude in the midst of community. Community here means a support and sustaining faith group, such as Lay Cistercians of Holy Spirit Monastery, Conyers, Ga. and Good Shepherd faith community at daily Mass and Liturgy of the Hours, with its ministries to the poor, the sick and those in need. Where two or three gather in my name, says the Master, there I am also.

3. Work to share my writings and adult learning about Cistercian spiritual practices.

4. Be open to the possibility of the manifestibility of all being! What seems like a mouthful of marbles is actual a way of saying that I will be more conscious of loving God with my whole heart, my whole mind, and my whole soul and my neighbor as myself.

Spiritual Practices I use to sustain my center:
These practices are little nests I carve out of my routine, not because I need the discipline but because they place me in direct contact with the

mind and heart of Christ.

Eucharist – The Sacrament of unity with God through Christ Jesus with the Holy Spirit as Advocate. This is the bread of Heaven. This is the pure energy of God for my transformation. This is my destiny in one prayer of gratitude with the community of believers.

Lectio Divina—This ancient, monastic practice allows me to growing deeper in spiritual awareness, there are four steps. Read (lectio); Meditate (meditatio); Pray (oratio); Contemplate (contemplatio).

Meditation and Spiritual Reading: This practice give me a time to focus on Scriptures, Spiritual Readings about how to grow deeper in Christ Jesus.

The Rosary: Meditations on the life and purpose of Christ Jesus One of my favorite practices is this mantra-like prayer to help me meditate on the highpoints in the life of Jesus.

Liturgy of the Hours: This practice, refined by St. Benedict in 580 AD in his Rule of St. Benedict, organizes the monks to pray the Psalms seven times a day. I pray the Psalms at least twice a day. The key is consistency and prayer in common, if possible. It is the prayer of the Catholic Church every hour of the day, every day of the week, giving praise, honor and glory to the Father through the Son in union with the Holy Spirit.

Eucharistic Adoration before the Blessed Sacrament: I believe that Jesus Christ is present, body and blood, soul and divinity, under the appearance of the bread. This is an ancient practice and one of the most revered of all practices. If this is indeed the living Christ, why would you not want to visit? This takes fierce love to practice.

Reading Chapter 4 or some part of the Rule of St. Benedict every day. By reading Chapter 4 each day, I hope to become what I read.

How I organize my daily practices:
>Horarium: (This is the default schedule of my spiritual practice.)
>4:00 a.m. Rise
>4:10 a.m. Silent Prayer

Morning Offering and Dedication of the Day

Monday: In reparation for my sins and those of the Church, those on my prayer list

Tuesday: For all family, friends, teachers, those on my prayer list

Wednesday: In honor of the Sacred Heart of Jesus, Immaculate Heart of Mary, and St. Joseph, those on my prayer list

Thursday: For all Lay Cistercians, Monks of Holy Spirit Monastery, Monks of St. Meinrad Archabbey, priests and religious of Diocese of Evansville, Monks of Norcia, Italy and those on my prayer list

Friday: For an increase in grace to love God with all my heart, all my soul, all my mind and my neighbor as myself.

Saturday: For all deceased, an increase in my faith through the Holy Spirit and for those on my prayer list.

Sunday: To give praise, honor and glory to the Father through the Son my means of the Holy Spirit, the God who is, was, and is to come at the end of the ages

4:30 a.m. Liturgy of the Hours: Readings in private (optional)
5:00 a.m. Exercise (Monday through Friday)
6:30 a.m. Breakfast:
7:40 a.m. Liturgy of the Word at Good Shepherd
    Morning Prayer in common
    Rosary in common
9:00 a.m. Holy Mass: In common (Sunday at 8:00 a.m.)
1:00 a.m. Exercise at gym: (Monday through Sunday)
11: 15 a.m. Work: Writing, Blog, Special Projects
12:00 a.m. Watch Colin Cowherd on television FX1
2:00 p.m. Work: Writing, Blog, Special Projects

4:30-5:30 p.m. Adoration before Blessed Sacrament in common
    Lectio Divina and Meditation in private
    Liturgy of the Hours: Evening Prayer in common
5:30 p.m. Supper
6:00-8:00 p.m. Exercise, Work, Read.
8:00 p.m. Liturgy of the Hours: Night Prayer in private (optional)
8:30 p.m. Work: Continue writing, Blog, Special Projects

WHAT I HAVE NOTICED ABOUT MYSELF SINCE MAKING A SCHEDULE AND KEEPING IT

- I don't always keep the schedule perfectly, but I always have it as a North on my compass of daily practice.
- I look forward to spending more time with Christ and less time with television, newspapers, listening to hateful news, and other distractions that the world has to offer.
- You don't need to fill in the daily schedule all at once. Pick out just one prayer practice (e.g. Lectio Divina) and try it every day for 30 days. At the end of that time evaluate yourself on a) your daily prayer; b) what you experienced by sitting next to the heart of Christ.
- I look forward to Lectio Divina, Eucharist, Liturgy of the Hours, Rosary, Private Prayer rather than have keeping the schedule be the end in itself.

SUSTAINING CONTEMPLATIVE SPIRITUALITY: DESIGN YOUR CONTEMPLATIVE SPIRITUAL SUPPORT SYSTEM

This section will help you design your own Contemplative spiritual system. Use this template to create your default spiritual system. Fill in the blanks.These six questions with corresponding answers are the foundation of spirituality, but they are not spirituality itself. What follows is your application of what you have learned about Cistercian spirituality to how you will live out the rest of your life, no matter how long or short that may be.

SOME TIPS ABOUT MAKING THIS SCHEDULE

- Don't make the mistake of thinking that making this schedule will make you a contemplative person. It won't. This is just one way that you can organize your thinking to give you the ability to focus every day on having in you the mind of Christ Jesus (Phil 2:5)

- You don't have to fill out all of the blanks below, especially the schdeule. I recommend you start off my just doing one think every day. My preference is reading Chapter 4 of St. Benedict's Rule, then Lectio Divina.

- If you don't do what you say, start over the try to keep it. Make all things new.

- You are not trying to be a Lay Cistercian but just someone who want to use silence and solitude as a way to meet Christ in your heart.
- You have just completed the six foundational questins for your spirituality. Now, what do you do for the rest of your life?

My Center:_____

My spiritual goals for the rest of my life: (Don't put anything down that you do not intend to do.)

1. _____

2. _____

3. _____

4 _____

Write down the Contemplative spiritual practices you will use to sustain your faith.

1._____
2._____
3._____
_____
4._____
5._____
6._____
7._____

How I organize my practices (See examples above)
Themes for each day:
Monday:_____
_____
Tuesday:_____
_____
Wednesday: _____
_____
Thursday: _____
_____
Friday: _____
_____
Saturday: _____
_____

Write down one or two practices you will attempt every day.

END NOTES FROM THE EDGE OF TIME
THE FINAL EXERCISE FOR THE MIND

In the space below, sum up all of your six questions that you have answered into one sentence. Take some time to think about your answer. It is not as easy as it seems. You began this book with the first question, what is the purpose of life? This was a macro answer, the 50,000 foot level of reality. Subsequent questions kept narrowing and sharpening your thoughts. This last question is the 5 foot level. What one sentence sums up the totality of your life. Can you do it? I can and did. I will share it, if you ask.

_____
_____
_____
_____
_____
_____
_____
_____
_____

BOOKS AND THINKERS THAT HAVE SHAPED MY SPIRITUAL AWARENESS

Many books have been assimilated into this brain and may still be in there, rattling around somewhere. Here are ten books that have helped me develop a hypothesis about what is real and how it all fits together. (In no order of importance)

1. Man's Search for Meaning

https://www.psychologytoday.com/blog/hide-and-seek/201205/mans-search-meaning

2. The Little Prince

http://www.angelfire.com/hi/littleprince/frames.html

3. The Phenomenon of Man

https://archive.org/details/ThePhenomenonOfMan

4. The Art of Loving

http://pdf-objects.com/files/ErichFromm_TheArtOfLoving

_1956_148pp.pdf
5. Six Thresholds of Life https:thecenterforcontemplativepractice.org
6. I-Thou and I-It http://www.newworldencyclopedia.org/entry/I-Thou
7. A Brief History of Time by Stephen Hawking
https://en.wikipedia.org/wiki/A_Brief_History_of_Time
8. The Cistercian Way by Dom Andre Louf, O.C.S.O.
https://www.amazon.com/Cistercian-Way-Studies-76/dp/0879079762
9. The Liturgy of the Hours https://divineoffice.org/welcome/
10. New Jerusalem Bible

List four books that have influenced your life. They don't have to be spiritual ones, but they should be book that have shaped how you think about purpose, your purpose, what reality looks like, how all reality fits together, how to love fiercely, and what you are going to do to prepare for death.

FINAL REFLECTION: TO WONDER OR WANDER, THAT IS THE QUESTION

I would like to share with you one of my Lectio Divina meditations (Phil 2:5) which deals with wonder. Having a background in scientific methodology (B.S. in Biology),. I used to wonder about the physical universe and how we humans even made it this far in the evolutionary chair. It is remarkable we have not killed ourselves, although it looks like we are trying hard to do so. The most recent encyclopedia from Pope Francis, Laudato Si (in Latin) confirms that, like Adam and Eve, God made all of us gardeners in the His garden. Some of us don't see it that way, but Pope Francis reminds us we are indeed stewards of God's landscape and will have to answer for our stewardship. Read it at:

http://w2.vatican.va/content/francesco/en/encyclicals/documents/papa-francesco_20150524_enciclica-laudato-si.html

I think that there are two approaches to contemplative spirituality (without trying to be overly simplistic,) The first is one of being someone who wonders about the world in which we live. We ask not only the questions of what is is, why is it and how is it (physical univese) but also what does it mean and where does everything fit (physical and mental universes)? Some of us go an extra step and ask what our purpose is, what is our purpose, and what does it mean to love fiercely (physical, mental and spiritual universes). The second way of thinking is that of a wonderer. I like to think of this type of wonderer as one who is able to look into the depths of his or her inner self and discover meaning as they approach the Mystery of Faith, the great cloud of unknowing. Read the full document at the following site:
https://www.catholicspiritualdirection.org/cloudunknowing.pdf

REFLECTIONS FROM A WONDERER

There some mysteries in the physical world and the mental world that I don't quite get. It is not that they are unknowabl, but that humans have not put all the pieces of the puzzle together yet. We are working on it. The same is true for the Mystery of Faith, that great unknowable called Heaven, or God, or Trinity. We know but what we don't know is greater. If I don't wonder about the world, the mind, and the Mystery of

Faith, I am condemned to wander in the wasteland of "what ifs" forever Here are some of the things I wonder about. What I write below are questions that I would ask, if I just believed in two universes (physical and mental). The answers I have for these questions of wonder are answered by the spiritual universe, specifically by Christ Jesus.

QUESTIONS OF WONDER
Like the Fermi Paradox, I wonder why we have not yet discovered any lifeforms out there, much less sentient ones?
https://www.space.com/25325-fermi-paradox.html
The article I read on the subject give all kinds of plausible explanation for Enrico Fermi's statement, "Where is everybody?" One thing they do not talk about is my concern, "What if there are no other sentient beings out there? Wonder if we *are* all alone in the cosmos? What are the implications in that? Scietifically, I know that the odds of that happening are low. Dr. Frank Drake even designed an equation to show the probability of life "out there." Here is is for those who like sources.
http://www.astrodigital.org/astronomy/drake_equation.html

That brings me to my second concern, "We are not made for space travel, so why are we so hell bent on doing the impossible?" You may not agree with this hypothesis, and some of my thinking is just to push against those who are too quick to dismss a spiritual reason. Think about it. We make much ado about space exploration with the certainty that no human could ever reach the nearest star in their own lifetime, and even if they did, what effects would the principle of genetic evolution have on those who survive? These are questions worth asking, even if the answers are obvious, depending which side of the life beyond earth you sit. Doesn't make sense!

It bothers me that people write about time without confronting the question of when it began or how it began or even why it began. It must be too obvious, which is why I don't get it. Doesn't make sense! Can you have matter and energy without time? Can you have a Heaven without time (as we know it). Must time exist in physical time? Is there such a thing as spiritual time? You must read my book, <u>The Woman Who Changed Time: Spirituality and Time</u>. It will take you to places you have never been before.

I wonder about the evolution of the human brain and why only humans have evolved with the capability to choose good from evil, all other things equal? All other speies can choose what is good from what is bad for them. Ask B.F. Skinner about choosing what is good and what is bad. They always choose what is good. A dog usually is centered around food its whole life, at least my dog, Tucker, does. Why can't a dog answer the question, "Tucker, can you meet me on Tuesday at Oliver Garden for lunch at 11:00 a.m.?" and "Do you know what the Original Sin of Adam and Eve is and why it is important for human behavior?" To be honest, I have some friends and colleagues who could not answer that last question. You get the point! We have reason for a reason. We have the ability to choose good from evil for a reason. We also know that humans do not determine what is good or evil, only God. The problem comes when people think everyone that has the right to choose what they want and that everything they choose is right because they choose it.

Is our human ability to choose linked to the archetypal choice Adam and Eve made to select themselves or recognize god is God? Read Genesis 2:16-17. This one of two traditions about trees has to do with the eating of the tree of the knowledge of good and evil. These ancient, oral traditions tease open for us the difference between humans and all other living things as part of a story of first choice. Is this part of a larger, more intricate plan of fulfillment of which we are not completely aware? Seems so simple on the surface is actually a complex reality that we today still have a problem defining to our satisfaction.

I wonder if humans have reason, as far as we know it, for a reason. If so, what reason would there be for me to make choices that impact my interface with reality now and for the future?

I wonder why God allows us to choose to love Him or not. Would anyone who actually saw God as He is, knowing that we would live forever with Him in perfect harmony of the Garden of Eden, ever choose not to be there? Unlikely! God chose to work through nature, allowing us to evolve through the crucible of extinctions and natural low, or not. Our moral thinking of what is good or evil comes from the natural law.

I wonder why there is sin in the world, sin meaning we humans do dumb things that "miss the mark" of what it means to be human. And who tells us about what is natural and what misses the mark? God tells us and later on Jesus shows us, and even later on, the Holy Spirit guides us by the Universal Church he founded to last until the last bang of the Big Bang.

I wonder why so many people who think they know about God, about what Christ intended for us, are based on their certitude that they represent God and are right, rather than on mercy and how to love one another as Christ loves us. Don't figure!

I wonder why there is only one truth but that many humans have the tower of Bable approach to god by thinking they possess the knowledge of the tree of good and evil. All religions have the temptation to do so.

I wonder why the three great sins of our age, modern idolatry (I am god, the center of all reality), relativism (everyone is their own god), and secularism (God is not relevant in my freedom to choose), have seduced all the nations of Humans, the learned and the weak of will to the exclusion of the Way, the Truth, and the Life. The cornerstone, once again, has been rejected, replaced by each of us, until we combust into dust in the span of our short lifetime.

I wonder how long it will be before we experience another Sodom and Gomorrah event, how long God will tolerate our foolishness,

how long will He let us continue down the path of self-destruction as a race? Our hope is in the name of the Lord and we must continuously ask his mercy on the dysfunction of the nations for turning away from His will. Read what the Pslamist says about his generation. Nothing is new,

Psalm 80 (NRSVCE)
Prayer for Israel's Restoration

Give ear, O Shepherd of Israel,   you who lead Joseph like a flock!
You who are enthroned upon the cherubim, shine forth   before Ephraim and Benjamin and Manasseh.
Stir up your might,   and come to save us!
Restore us, O God; let your face shine, that we may be saved.
O Lord God of hosts, how long will you be angry with your people's prayers?
You have fed them with the bread of tears, and given them tears to drink in full measure.

You make us the scorn of our neighbors; our enemies laugh among themselves.
Restore us, O God of hosts; let your face shine, that we may be saved.

It bothers me that I am not perfect. Each day is a lifetime. I must practice my Faith as lived out as a Lay Cistercian every single day, making things new every morning. The effects of Original Sin, the temptations, the roller coaster ride of human emotions and feelings all take their toll on my Spirit. I am a broken, down, old, Temple of the Holy Spirit, cracked and with many vines growing. Through it all, I am called to prefer nothing to the love of Christ (Chapter 4 of the Rule of St. Benedict)

Write down some of the wonders you have about the life you lead. Are there inconsistencies? Are there challenges yet to be discovered?

Notes:

ADDITIONAL RESOURCES THAT HAVE HELPED ME ON MY LAY CISTERCIAN JOURNEY (SO FAR)

Here are some wonderful, contemplative websites in which you may find some rest for your soul. I admit my bias.

http://www.trappist.net
http://www.newadvent.com
https://thecenterforcontemplativepractice.org
http://www.cistercianfamily.org/
https://siena.org/
http://www.carlmccolman.net
http://scotthahn.com
http://www.cistercianpublications.org
http://dynamiccatholic.com
http://www.centeringprayer.com/cntrgpryr.htm
http://www.monk.org
https://cistercianpublications.org/Category/CPCT/Cistercian-Tradition
http://www.saintmeinrad.edu
http://w2.vatican.va/content/vatican/en.html
http://ccc.usccb.org/flipbooks/catechism/files/assets/basic-html/page-I.html#
http://www.catholicapologetics.org/
https://stpaulcenter.com/support-the-center
https://www.osv.com/Home.aspx
http://www.osb.org/cist/
http://www.usccb.org/beliefs-and-teachings/how-we-teach/catechesis/catechetical-sunday/word-of-god/upload/lectio-divina.pdf
http://www.ewtn.com/library/mary/bernard2.htm
https://www.ecatholic2000.com/index2.html
https://www.youtube.com/watch?v=p_shhU_H5Z0
https://www.youtube.com/watch?v=1sfMYn3YcT8
https://www.youtube.com/watch?v=UYE7CC1m_II
https://cistercianfamily.org/lay-groups/

THE CHRIST IMPERATIVES

LISTEN TO ME, FOR I AM MEEK AND HUMBLE OF HEART.
Matthew 11:28-30

- Thirsty? Drink of the living waters! John 7:37.
- Hungry? Eat the food that gives eternal life! John 6:33-38.
- Bewildered? Believe in the Master! John 3:11-21.
- Without hope? Be not afraid! John 13:33-35.
- Lost? Find the way. John 14:6-7.
- Tired because of the pain? Be renewed! John 15:1-7.
- Afraid? Find peace! John 27-28.
- Afraid to believe? Believe! John 11:25-27.
- Without a family? Listen! John 10:7-18.
- In darkness? Walk in the light! John 8:12.
- Spiritually depressed? Be healed! John 5:24

Welcome, good and faithful servant, into the Kingdom, prepared for you before the world began.

THE CONTEMPLATIVE PRACTICE SERIES

1. SPIRITUAL APES: Our Journey to Forever, Vol. I.
2. SPIRITUAL APES: Our Journey from Animality to Spirituality, Vol II.
3. SPIRITUAL APES: The Struggle to Be Spiritual, Vol. III.
4. HOW TO GRIEVE WELL. What Happens to You When You Have Lost Loved One? Spirituality for the Bereaved.
5. What Happens to You When You Have Lost a Pet? Spirituality for Pet Owners.
6. HOW TO DIE WELL. So You Know You Are Going to Die, Now What? A Spiritual Preparation for Life...Forever.
7. Have You Lost All Your Marbles...or Just Your EX? Spiritual Perspectives for Divorced Women
8. Searching for Love in the Garden of Eden. Spirituality for the Lonely of Heart.
9. If Life is a Journey, Have You Lost the Road Map? Spiritual Toolkit for Divorced Men.
10. Spiritual Estate Planning: Can the Rich Get to Heaven?
11. Is Your Spiritual Life Running on Empty? Overcoming Spiritual Depression.
12. Resolving Spiritual Conflicts:101 Ways Split-Religion Moms and Dads Can Agree.
13. How Moms and Dads Can Be Spiritual Directors: Developmental Spirituality.
14. Who Does God Think He Is, Anyway? Guidance from the Master.
15. The Woman Who Changed Time: Spirituality and Time.
16. You Are My Heritage: A Father's Thoughts as His Daughter Enters College.
17. 17 Skills Moms and Dads Must Teach Their Children: Show Your Children How to Get to Heaven.
18. Who Rows Your Boat? How to Be Happier Than You Can Possibly Imagine.
19. Three Rules of the Spiritual Universe: How to Choose an Authentic Center That Leads to Heaven.

20. Six Thresholds of Life: How to prepare to live…Forever. Participant Workbook.
21. Facilitating Adult Learning: How to facilitate The Center for Contemplative Practice workshops.
22. Come, Share Your Lord's Joy: A Journal to Prepare for Life…Forever.
23. Spiritual Estate Planning: A Journal to Build Spiritual Wealth You Can Take to Heaven.
24. You Are My Heritage: Thoughts on How Much You Mean to Me.
25. The Center of My Life: Thoughts on the Assumptions Underlying What I Believe.
26. How to Stop Assumicide. How to Think Critically About What You Believer, Without Destroying Your Faith.
27. Mining for Heavenly Gold While On Earth: How to Center Yourself on What Is Authentic.
28. Five Steps to Build a Better Future for Your Community: What should your community look like in the future?
29. Resolving Spiritual Conflicts: Spirituality for Split-Religion Moms and Dads
30. HOW TO DIE WELL: You know you are going to die, now what? Tabletop Exercises for Facilitators in Adult Learning Centers, Book One
31. HOW TO GRIEVE WELL: What happens to you when you have lost a loved one? Tabletop Exercises for Facilitators in Adult Learning Centers, Book Two
32. You Know You Are Going to Die, Now What? A cancer survivor reflets on how contemplation helps confront three question you must face head on: A Journal.
33. The Lay Cistercian Spiritual Journey: A Lay Cistercian reflects on a document about the call, his response, community, formation and transformation into The Life of Christ.
34. Six Thresholds of Life: How to prepare to live…Forever.
35. You Know You Are Going to Die, Now What? A Lay Cistercian cancer survivor reflects on Three Questions he had to face head on and how contemplation helped him discover peace, joy, and love.

36. contemplative thremes that increase "capacitas dei: making room for God in you.
37. Prayer: Messages from the Edge of Time. A Lay Cistercian reflects on two dimensions of prayer.
38. Spirituality for Atheists, Agnostics, and Pagans: A Lay Cistercian reflects on six questions each of us must answer before we die.
39. Seeking God in Daily Living: A Lay Cistercian reflects on five contemplative practices to move from self to God.
40. Messages from the Edge of Time: A Lay Cistercian reflects on six photographic themes for visual learners that lead to converting self to God
41. For Behold, I Make All Things New: A Lay Cistercian reflects on Mercy, Forgiveness, Confession and Penance to grow in faith, love and service.

BLOG

https://thecenterforcontemplativepractice.org

WHAT IS THE CENTER FOR CONTEMPLATIVE PRACTICE?
The Center for Contemplative Practice is a ministry of people devoted to providing spiritual resources for adults, such as publishing books, retreats, training, blogs, and online meditations on Cistercian practices.

DISCLAIMER The ideas and meditations contained in any books or blogs shared by The Center for Contemplative Practice do not represent the official, authoritative teaching of the Roman Catholic Church or any Cistercian Monastery or Lay Cistercian group. These ideas and are the results of Lectio Divina spiritual meditations by the author and reflect only his interpretation of Catholic, spiritual thoughts through contemplation.

ABOUT THE AUTHOR
Michael F. Conrad, B.S., M.R.E., Ed.D., is retired from a full life of trying to make money, seek fame and recognition by the world, all without much success. Coming to his senses, even after the age of 78, he now struggles to keep in him the mind of Christ Jesus. (Philippians 2:512) Still running the race and searching for the prize, he has had a lifetime of activities to help him in his quest: he is proud to have been a U.S. Army Chaplain, pastor of parish ministry, adjunct instructor of Adult Education at Indiana University (Bloomington) and University of South Florida (Tampa) and Barry University (Florida), high school instructor of religion, trainer of managers and supervisors, adjunct trainer for the Florida Certified Public Manager program, instructional designer for the State of Florida, former Florida Supreme Court Certified Family Mediator, and currently a publisher, blogger, and author, He is a Lay Cistercian member of Our Lady of the Holy Spirit Monastery, Conyers, Georgia, proud father of a daughter, and a humbled husband.

What follows is a poem about my life. It is, as yet, unfinished as is my life, but the elements are all present.

The Poem of My Life

I sing the song of life and love...
   …sometimes flat and out of tune
   …sometimes eloquent and full of passion
   …sometimes forgetting notes and melody
   …sometimes quaint and intimate
   …often forgetful and negligent
   …often in tune with the very core of my being
   …often with the breath of those who would pull me down, shouting right in my face
   …often with the breath of life uplifting me to heights never before dreamed
   …greatly grateful for the gift of humility and obedience to The One
   …greatly thankful for adoption, the discovery of new life of pure energy
   …greatly appreciative for sharing meaning with others of The Master
   …greatly sensitive for not judging the motives of anyone but me
   …happy to be accepted as an aspiring Lay Cistercian
   …happy to spend time in Eucharistic Adoration
   …happy and humbled to be an adopted son of the Father
   …happy for communities of faith and love with wife, daughter, friends
   …mindful that the passage of time increases each year
   …mindful of the major distractions of cancer and cardiac arrest
   …mindful of my center and the perspective that I am loved moreover, I must love back with all the energy of my heart and strength, yet always falling a little short
   …mindful the energy I receive from The One in Whom I find Purpose and meaning…Forever.

To The One who is, Who was, and Who is to come at the end of the ages, be glory, honor, power, and blessings through The Redeemer Son in unity with the Advocate, Spirit of Love.

From The One who is, Who was, and Who is to come at the end of the ages, I seek hope that His words about the purpose of life are true, that He is the way that leads to life…Forever.

With The One who is, Who was, and Who is to come at the end of the ages, I seek fierce love so I can have in me the mind of Christ Jesus, my purpose in life and my center…Forever.

"That in all things, may God be glorified." –St. Benedict

Made in the USA
Columbia, SC
10 July 2019

MARITAL INTIMACY